How to be a Successful

Related titles:

Susan Tranter and Adrian Percival: *How to Run your School Successfully*

Chris Turner: *How to Run your Department Successfully*

Michael Marland and Rick Rogers: *How to be a Successful Form Tutor*

Jean Rudduck and Julia Flutter: *How to Improve Your School*

Helen Gunter: *Leading Teachers*

How to be a Successful Deputy Head

Geoff Brookes

continuum
LONDON • NEW YORK

Continuum International Publishing Group
The Tower Building   80 Maiden Lane
11 York Road   Suite 704
London   New York
SE1 7NX   NY 10038

British Library Cataloguing-in-Publication Data
A catalogue record for this book is available from the British Library.

ISBN: 0–8264–8646–0 (hardback)
      0–8264–8647–9 (paperback)

Library of Congress Cataloging-in-Publication Data
A catalog record is available from the Library of Congress.

Typeset by Ben Cracknell Studios

Printed and bound in Great Britain by MPG Books Ltd,
Bodmin, Cornwall.

Contents

Acknowledgements

When Christina and Alexandra at Continuum told me the title of this book I was alarmed. I know how to be a deputy head. I do it every day. I put my suit on, go to school and upset as many people as possible. But a successful one? I wasn't sure about that. That is a judgement that others must make. As a deputy all you can ever be is a representative of the community where you work. They are the ones who will judge whether or not you are successful. I hope this book will help you to work out how to become one.

I must thank all my colleagues in Cefn Hengoed Community School where I have learned how to do the job. Their patience with my mistakes and my – sometimes – peculiar decisions has been the secure framework within which I have been able to work happily with both staff and students. I have been the longest serving deputy in the school's history. A successful one? I hope so.

I should like to thank my friend Jane Whitmore who has formatted the forms and tables that have been used as illustrations in this book. Please feel free to use them or adapt them as you wish.

I must also thank *The Times Educational Supplement* who have shown unwarranted faith in my writing. The sections on Exclusion, Medical needs and Dealing with parents have been adapted from pieces I wrote for Jill Craven at *Friday* magazine, which is part of the *TES*.

Your success in your job will, however, depend more than anything else upon the love and support you have at home. I have always had these things and I would neither have done the job nor have written this book without them.

And you never know, my wife Liz might well be right – living with a deputy head is much harder than being one.

Acknowledgments

Introduction

I dallied – briefly – with the idea of becoming a headteacher. I applied for a couple of posts and went for an interview. I got down to the last three. But I wasn't at all surprised that I wasn't appointed. I knew I hadn't been convincing. I hadn't been able, at any stage, to project myself into the role.

I knew at that point that being a deputy head was what I was meant to be. In my career I have seen what a good head can do and also what effect a poor one can have. I wasn't confident what sort of head I would become. I decided it was better to remain as a competent deputy rather than risk everything and then fail. By so doing I would have damaged my own sense of self-worth and seriously affected the careers of others. It wasn't worth the risk.

I also realized something else: that I was not ready to leave teaching behind. I was not ready to embrace the loneliness of a head's job.

Of course some people are ready to accept those challenges but I wasn't sure that I could deliver. It was a decision that I have not, as yet, regretted. As a result I have built up a body of experience about the role of the deputy, which I am grateful to have the opportunity to share. This experience is at the heart of this book. It is based upon the 14 years I have spent – so far – as deputy headteacher of Cefn Hengoed Community School in Swansea. Seek the school out on the Internet. It will tell you everything you might need to know about us. We are an ordinary comprehensive school, serving a challenging area. Just like most schools. Some things we do well; in other things we are less convincing. Just like most schools. We remain largely unknown, though we are a special place to all of us who go there. Just like most schools.

And I suppose that is all I can offer the reader of this book. A perspective from an ordinary school, for better and for worse.

In writing this book I realized quickly that there are some issues that I couldn't deal with. I have tried to avoid the specifics of an ever-changing educational world. We have a way of giving new names to old ideas in education. We drag old clothes from a box in the attic and call them something new in an attempt to make them trendy and fashionable. Rather like flared trousers. Any attempt to maintain the present currency of linguistic gymnastics when talking about schools would lock this book into a particular place in time. When flared trousers were or were not in fashion. If I included too much detail that is contemporary to me as I sit at my computer in 2005, it would certainly help to make this book obsolescent very quickly. This book is designed to deal with principles and practices of managing a school today, whenever today is. I rely upon you, the reader, to be fully informed of all current developments. After all, that is part of your job isn't it? There we are – an early example of delegation. It's easy when you know how. Your experience so far will have shown you that schools are such complex organisms. There are so many different individuals interacting in an unpredictable way on a daily basis that as institutions they are extremely volatile and endlessly surprising. Are two days ever alike? Not in my experience.

The fundamentals however never change. You put teachers in a classroom with students and you then manage the consequences. Dress it up in any way you like to reflect the vocabulary of a new generation, but this basic element remains unchallenged.

So who is this book for? It is for those who aspire to the post and who are looking for a way to prepare themselves for its challenges. It is for newly appointed deputies who are feeling their way into a very challenging role. It is for existing deputies who are looking to reflect on their performance by reading with a sense of recognition and of disagreement And it is also for headteachers who can read it and so remind themselves of what it is that they are missing. I hope all of you find it useful. And I hope all of you enjoy it.

Why the job is important

There is no other job in a secondary school that is anything like being a deputy head. The job is completely unpredictable. Some people thrive on this, whilst others are unsettled by its uncertainty. There can be no doubt that you will be at the centre of what goes on in the school, perhaps even more so than the head.

You see, the head leads. The head provides the strategic overview, the vision. They are the figurehead, standing at the prow in a noble posture, shielding their eyes from the sun and scanning the far horizon. Artists want to paint their picture.

Meanwhile, you are sweating down below with the galley slaves, beating the drum. It is your job to make sure that the school reaches those distant shores. Few portrait painters are brave enough to confront the nether world below decks.

Of course this is simplistic. In these days of leadership teams, roles are not so carefully defined. But, certainly, what you do isn't entirely separated from the concerns of a classroom teacher in the way that a headteacher's role is separated. You will work closely with both students and teachers. A head can do a perfectly good job and yet find themselves separated from these things.

I know that it may be obvious, but this is not a job for anyone who doesn't like children. If you don't like the classroom then you shouldn't be a teacher, let alone a deputy. And don't apply to become a deputy because you believe that it is a desk job. It is not a job for anyone who wants to hide. Every aspect of the school's daily life will somehow end up on your desk. On really bad days I can't help thinking that the things no one else fancies doing are thrown in my direction. Awkward parents, problems with the buses, issues over exam invigilation, a survey from a professional association, an odd phone call from the police. I get a chance to do it all. Come and join me. Essentially if it walks down the drive or comes in the post it will be yours and you will be expected to do something about it and not make a mistake.

This is why the job is both exhausting and exciting. Nothing happens that you don't know about. In fact, you may decide not to share some of these things with the headteacher since they are not important enough for their attention. But nothing is too insignificant for yours.

So is the job about maintenance rather than development? Of course not. It would be a poor job indeed if all you did was deal with the nuts and bolts of the day. You will be involved in setting the tone and the direction of your school. But there can be no doubt that your job will keep you in touch with the staffroom and the classroom and all those other places in between.

Managing a school is a unique experience because schools are different from other places. Their essential unpredictability makes them attractive places for many outside education. You may occasionally yearn for the certainties of a desk job and an organized pile of papers to process. But those who have made that their career, yearn for the excitement and randomness of schools.

This is largely because schools are about people. Whatever else you forget in your career, never forget that the job you have is about students and the way that they hope to build their lives. It is your job to facilitate learning. You might well spend your time managing people and resources and developing systems, but never forget why you do it. Everything else is fluff. Don't forget that either. Schools exist, not for teachers, but for students. It is your job to manage and deploy resources to make this happen. You will do this because you will command a unique position, one slippery but important rung up the evolutionary ladder.

You see, you are an amphibian. You live in the swamp with the teachers but you also inhabit the higher ground with the more highly evolved. As a result you may find that you belong in neither place. You may find that your idealism is replaced by pragmatism. You may find that your working life becomes frenetic. But one thing is clear. None of it will ever be dull.

PART ONE

What you have to be

1 What do the adverts say?

Lead from the front. Don't lurk at the back

There are always adverts for deputy head jobs throughout the country. People are always moving on and so creating vacancies. And they are important vacancies. It is a very important appointment for a governing body. They will have considered very carefully what it is that they are looking for. The advertisement is a considerable expense for any school, and they shouldn't enter into the marketplace until they are absolutely certain about what they want. So when you see an advert don't dismiss the content out of hand and regard it as irrelevant. It can't be. If you believe that any deputy head job anywhere is desirable, then you probably won't make a good one. It should never be the case that any appointment will do. The position should never be regarded as a stepping stone to something else. It should be an end in itself. There should be a match between yourself and the institution. You have to fit in with the precise details of the specification. Don't ever think that you would like to become a deputy simply because you want more money. Of course the money is nice, but such a motivation can only ever lead to dissatisfaction when you finally reach a point at which no more money is available.

You need to want to do the job because you have something to offer a particular school on the basis of what you have done and what you believe. And if we look at the advertisements themselves, they will give you a clear idea of the general qualities you will need to show. This is a good place to start because it tells us what people believe they are looking for. These are the things that are expected of you. It is good to consider them now and again, whether you are looking for such a post for the first time or if you already have this coveted job. After a bad day it is good to be reminded of the qualities other people believe you possess, and the sort of leadership you have to go back into school and show tomorrow.

In the first place adverts ask for 'proven classroom skills'. This can't be a surprise. Teachers want to be led by good teachers who can act as role models, as well as show that they are good managers. You certainly don't become a deputy head in order to escape from the classroom. Far from it. After a significant period of success you will feel able to operate at a whole-school level, offering your skills to a range of other colleagues. You will be passing judgement on them. They need to be reassured that you can do it yourself. So you must be good. Nothing else will do.

Adverts might indicate that they want you to have 'significant experience'. What does this mean? How long should you have been teaching? This is difficult, for there is no hard and fast rule. All one can say is that it is probably important that you have had experience of a number of different situations and positions in school. As a result, you have something to offer a school and other teachers who might, indeed, have had more years in the classroom than yourself. Your experience needs to be relevant too, and substantial. It is not enough to be able to count efficiently the rulers in the mathematics department.

A governing body is also looking for enjoyment – enjoyment both of teaching and of learning. You need to enjoy your subject and your work and enjoy being in a school. You will need to show a commitment to the essential purposes of the job. The job has to mean something to you. Because if it does, then you will want to make sure that your school becomes a better place as a result of what you do.

Schools want 'good inter-personal skills'. Think about it. The colourless cold fish behind the computer is hardly going to inspire a generation of young people. As deputy you will be a significant person in the school career of all the students who spend time there. You will be a successful professional who can persuade and lead staff and students, not a desk jockey. Managing people will be the hardest thing that you do. You will be expected to articulate the vision of the school and communicate its values clearly and consistently.

The adverts often say that they are looking for someone 'committed to excellence'. In other words they want the promotion of high standards and the sense that their school is an important place, at the very least as good as other places and in reality so much better. They are looking for high standards, not only in the work produced but also in the way that the school presents itself. Students need to be a credit to their community, both when they are in it and when they are outside it. The governing body wants you to set standards and serve the needs of aspiring parents and communities. Remember, schools exist to help all students to achieve goals. You need to show your talents to promote such achievement.

A word you will commonly see is 'enthusiastic', the sort of quality that is destined to make you wildly unpopular in cynical staffrooms across the country. There is no getting away from it though. You have to show that the job is important to you, and that you believe in the school and its success. Leadership involves persuading people to do things that they don't always want to do. You will have to shepherd unwilling staff 'out of the comfort zone'. You will be expected to lead from the front, not from behind your paperclip dispenser.

Adverts will often indicate that they want someone who is 'ambitious'. By that they mean both personally ambitious and ambitious for the school and its students. The feeling is that in their ambition the successful candidate will innovate and move the school forward as an example of what they can do. Governing bodies might be reluctant to appoint if they knew that the candidate was likely to settle into the very fabric of the place and so prove resistant to change and progression. The argument isn't entirely convincing but certainly they are looking for someone with drive, ready and willing to take over in an acting capacity if it is necessary. This is a significant point. They are looking for headteacher material because you could in fact become one by default, through illness or unexpected departure. Suddenly the head-teacher will be you and the governors need to be confident that their school will not suddenly fall apart.

'A clear vision' is regarded as an important quality. Teachers can so easily become bogged down in the day-to-day management of the classroom and cannot always see beyond it. To be a deputy means you have got to have a sense of where your school needs to go and, more importantly, how to get there. Adverts might also say that they want someone to be part of a team in order to make these things happen. Fair enough. But the candidate will also need to be able to work independently.

The same words appear in many advertisements and you will have seen this yourself. If you are daunted by what they say, then you should realize that this is a step for which you are not yet ready. You can't bluff your way through an interview in the hope that somehow you can disguise the fact that the necessary skills are not yet in place. Deputy head is a demanding and high profile job and significant weaknesses will be ruthlessly exposed. Of course they want a lot from you. But you have a great deal to offer. It is probably instructive to look at what the *School Teacher's Pay and Conditions Document* says about the role. It certainly indicates that you are a special hybrid thing. You will carry out the professional duties of a teacher and also play a major role in directing the school. You will formulate aims and objectives and establish the policies through which they will be achieved. You will manage the staff and resources to make sure it happens and monitor progress to their achievement. There we are then. Easy isn't it. Oh and deputize for the headteacher when necessary. Not a problem. Oh yes, and can you see your way to learning two obscure foreign languages before breakfast? Thanks.

Once you have examined these much sought-after qualities, then perhaps the next stage is to send off for details from a range of schools. You don't have to apply for the jobs. Use the opportunity for personal professional development. You will get an insight into a wide range of schools across the country and as a result form a clearer idea of how you fit in.

Is there anything else you need to do in order to improve your profile? Apart from reading this book that is. It is important to be informed before you jump in. You need to know how deep the water is and where the sharks are before you go swimming in the sea.

Of course, it is not the purpose of this book to tell you about writing letters or developing interview techniques. The qualities you display will ensure that you succeed. These will be the things that impress. You have never been afraid of taking responsibility. You have never been afraid of making decisions. You are measured and decisive, committed and honourable. The appointments panel will recognize these things.

Above all else, be honest with the school and with yourself. Don't try and twist the truth in order to press the right buttons. You need to find a job in a school that is right for you and you should be right for the governing body. You will get the job because you are the best candidate and because that community feels that you have something to offer them. You must feel that it is an honour and a privilege to accept the post. If you don't feel like this then it is not the place for you. Withdraw from the interview. It is the honourable thing to do, and it stops you wasting everyone's time.

Your appointment is an achievement and one that you should be proud of. Celebrate it well. But of course, after the appointment, the real work then begins.

2   On arrival

Walk away from the phone. Ignore the papers on the desk

When you are first appointed the expectations are great. Everyone wants a new manager to sweep away the absurdities of the old regime – but only those they didn't like. Some absurdities they will want to preserve. They wouldn't want to see their own sinecures and privileges coming under threat. And, as a general rule, too much change too quickly is unsettling for many teachers. The prospect of their cosy little world suddenly transformed is especially daunting.

But of course, you were not appointed to leave things as they are. Initially, and only if it is possible, you should be measured in what you do. Take time to look around and assess the lie of the land. Something might happen which would force you to have an immediate impact and if those situations arise then you must not shirk them, for it is in such moments your influence could almost be defined forever. If a student is attacked with a brick on your first day then you have to act. That happened on my very first day in teaching and I was relieved that I didn't have to sort it out. But you can't wait for someone else to sort it out. Now it is your job. The way you deal with it will be analysed minutely.

If it is possible, it is more preferable to ease yourself into your new community. Introduce yourself to all the different elements within the school in turn. If you can manage it, this is often especially effective if carried out before you take up your post. They will feel especially favoured if you have travelled specially to meet them. You will meet the teachers and the students, obviously. But don't forget the cleaners and the catering staff, the PTA and the caretakers, and the lollipop operative and the local shop owner. Remember, you are now a figure within the local community.

So, in your first few days reflect and observe. You have been appointed for the long haul. Find out what is going on. Obviously you will need to be a visible presence right from the start. No staffroom wants to believe that they are being directed by a desk commander. So get into the yard, the dining room, assemblies. Lurk in the corridors – you'll find out as much there as you will from lesson observation – be there between the lessons. What you are doing is taking the temperature of the school, you are feeling the culture.

Walk away from the phone, the papers on the desk. Get out there and pick up a bit of litter. When you are out there you will be gathering information, along with the crisp packets. It is called 'Managing by Walking About' and it has a long and distinguished history. Then, when you feel you have got things sorted in your own head, start to introduce your schemes and initiatives. This is much more productive than the approach of the frantic nutter who sets up three working parties and alienates the whole of the science department before lunchtime on day one. But at the same time, you mustn't merely champion cosmetic change. A bit of painting in the staffroom and a refurbished toilet is undeniably a start, but it does not justify the size of your salary if what you do has no impact upon teaching and learning. Putting a coffee machine in the staffroom might be a real symbol of regime change, but you want to be remembered for more than that irritating rota on the staffroom notice board for the disposal of coffee grounds. Teachers are always quick to remind you that as a workforce they are neglected and that they need to be valued and you need to care for their needs and it isn't fair that . . . But remember that their needs must take second place to the needs of the students. If you try to base your appointment on fulfilling the needs of the staff, you will inevitably fail and you will be betraying your role and profession. The students come first.

A friend of mine made a particularly impressive impact by taking her time to assess her new school and then holding an assembly in which she gave her frank assessment of what she had seen and what needed to be done. She showed photos of the litter and graffiti problem around the school, she revealed data about internal truancy and behaviour. Then, when the issues had been defined, she indicated very clearly what she intended to do about it all. The school knew then what they had got. They knew why she had been appointed. They knew she intended to make a difference.

If you are appointed from within the school you have the advantage of knowing the place and the students. But it might be more difficult to establish that your role has changed. There will be those who have great expectations. They might believe that the fact they sat next to you in the staffroom entitles them to certain privileges. They might presume a relationship. Others might believe that previous rivalries mean that their department must now inevitably fall upon hard times. In both cases what you have to do is indicate that that was then, this is now. You are indeed a new you, with a new job and new purpose. What, of course, you can illustrate is commitment to the school and the community. You will have worked within it for some time and in different roles. But things have changed.

The staffroom is no longer your space, if it was before. Go in occasionally when you have to, but knock before you enter. The staff have a right to the privacy they need in which to slag you off. Friday night drinking sessions are out too, the possibilities for an indiscreet word, real and imagined, are just too great. At any social event, remember that now you are a different sort of beast. This is what makes an internal appointment trickier to deal with. If you come from outside the school, then you not only arrive with a fresh perspective, but also you leave most of this baggage behind you in your previous school. Everyone starts again. If you have been in the school for a while this is much more complicated.

Your relationships with colleagues will be another expression of staffroom politics. Let's be honest, it is important to some people that they have someone to dislike at work. It makes them feel better. That person is likely to be you. I think I can guarantee that there will be someone on your staff who will smile and smile and be a villain. They are everywhere.

Schools are not open-plan offices, a design adopted by those wishing to minimize office politics. There are plenty of rooms and offices for the secret vitriolic gossip that serves to bind parts of the organization together. It will happen. Never worry about it. You may see yourself as a man of the people who can offer a cheery word and a friendly hand on the shoulder, but can you really be sure that this is how they see you? Are those who have worked with you and know your occasional failings, ready to emphasize your more frequent successes? Or are they jealous? And can you deal with the sudden unpopularity you might experience? If this picture sounds too cynical then I might be persuaded to accept that I have overstated the case. I am allowed to as a writer. But do not think for a moment that there will not be teachers who will try to manipulate you. And if you are not ready for this and all the rest of the fall-out that comes from the job and the decisions you make, then you are not ready to be a deputy.

3   Now you are in post

Change your perspective

It is highly unlikely that your school will be a blank canvas. You will inherit practices and procedures, many of which will seem to have been there forever. In fact, their purpose will be quite simply that they have existed for a while. Remember that you can change them. This is why you were appointed. The governing body was prepared to back your judgement when they appointed you and the headteacher will welcome the freshness of your vision and the new perspective that you bring. It is certainly easier in this regard if you have been appointed from elsewhere. The issue for internal appointments is always that if you were unhappy with something, then why did you not try to change it before? Of course, it is not as simple as that, but it is definitely harder to make a change in your role and in the way that people perceive you if a couple of weeks before you were grumbling in the staffroom with everyone else.

Of course, even if you don't change things, you should bring your own style to the post. To some extent you will be regarded as a known quantity and quite possibly a safe and unthreatening option. But those opinions were formed only on your performance in your old role, not in your new one. In your new role you will be an entirely different animal.

It is all about changing your perspective. You can perform any number of new tasks that come with the role. You can work longer, move more paper, make longer lists. But you will not become a deputy head until you change your view. You must make the move in your own mind. Think about the whole, not the parts, think about direction and priorities. You need to concern yourself with intangibles, like tone and atmosphere. You need to be leading, not managing. There may have been elements of your previous job in school which were competitive, where you promoted your own department to obtain resources denied others. Now you need to have a broader perspective. You must support the weaker heads of department and compensate for poor leadership in order to maximize opportunities for the students. A failing department now reflects on you. You can neither hide nor shirk your responsibility. Once you know something then you have to act. You can't ignore it anymore or sit in the corner of the staffroom and shrug your shoulders. You are part of a leadership team that needs to find solutions and makes sure that they work.

You are paid to make decisions. Of course you must consult and take advice. You need to involve colleagues in the things that shape the direction of the school. They need to have a sense of ownership if developments are to be made to work. But your job goes beyond being merely a facilitator who discovers and then implements the majority view. If you are only ever going to take a consensus, then you are being paid too much. Change is implemented by individuals articulating a vision. You have to make decisions and sometimes they will be painful and unpopular. But this is what you are paid for. Without bravery and honesty, the job remains one merely of paper shuffling and lunch duty. It can come as quite a shock to new deputies to realize just how unpopular they can be with some colleagues. The job itself seems to inspire huge mounts of bile. You are seen to be someone who has been far too eager to escape the real work of the classroom. A careerist, ready to sacrifice anyone and anything in order to scramble to the top of the mud heap. Sometimes these attitudes are fuelled by envy. Don't forget that the job is desired by many and achieved by few. Sometimes teachers will project their own unhappiness in the classroom onto you. You became a deputy in order to avoid children, not to facilitate their learning. It is what they would do if they had the chance. They will see you as busy doing nothing, even when you are working the whole day through. Even if you have witnessed these reactions from the staffroom yourself, it is still a surprise when they are focused on to you. You have to accept it. Don't think that you will win everyone over so that spontaneous applause breaks out in the staffroom whenever you walk in. It is not going to happen. All you can hope for in some areas is to play out an honourable draw.

When you are first appointed your pleasure at your success will soon be replaced by a sense of apprehension. You will face the reality of what you have to do very quickly. If you have been a successful middle manager you will suddenly feel that you have sacrificed your sense of security. All you can do is be confident and be yourself. Then slowly you will be able to empower and lead others through your leadership. You have been selected by the governors and the head because of the qualities you have displayed. But you don't become a deputy just because a governing body grants you the title. You only are a deputy head when you are accepted as such in the minds of your teaching colleagues. This takes time, but you will get there if they can see your commitment, not to yourself, but to the school and its students. They may not agree with the decisions you make, but will accept that you are acting upon judgements that were professionally formed. They will accept you when you show you are reliable and decisive. They will accept you when you show you are committed and consistent. But, perhaps most importantly of all, they need to feel that you are honest and supportive.

What you need to do now is to consider how you are going to display these qualities.

4 Your day-to-day world

Everything is now your job

Much of what you will do will be trivial. But they are the things that keep your school ticking over. You can sometimes wonder how it came about that grown adults are unable to make even the most obvious decision. But the point is that someone has to make those decisions. Someone has to put their name on things. They are sheep awaiting instructions from a sheepdog. And that sheepdog is you. People know what has to be done – that classroom can't be used because the ceiling has fallen in. The answer is obvious. Move to another one. But the school requires you to make that decision. That is what you have to do.

At the same time, you will be involved in strategic planning, involving large sums of money, or with complex contractual issues for part-time French teachers. You are expected to see the bigger picture as well as the nitty-gritty. You will be expected to manage adults, teaching and non-teaching, colleagues and strangers, children, resources, buildings, stray animals. There is nothing that can happen in school that you can walk away from, saying, 'That's not my job.' Everything is your job. Perhaps the headteacher can wash their hands of certain issues (though it is not something to be recommended). But you can't. You can never walk away.

Oh, and by the way, in between you have to scuttle off to deliver quality lessons. This is what makes the job so unpredictable and so exhausting. One of the great sadnesses of being a deputy is that eventually some of us feel that we no longer have any skills at all. We spend all our time dealing with other people's issues, making decisions that are really compromises that please no one, teaching difficult classes, dealing with naughty students. It doesn't take long before your sense of your own abilities disappears. You may find that you lose track of developments in your own subject area. You may find that you are no longer teaching the sort of classes on which your reputation has been built. Instead of the certainties of your own classroom, you will become a beast of burden. As you walk around the school, teachers will give you another monkey to carry. They will have passed a problem on to you that has thus made their life a little easier. But it has made yours that little bit more complicated.

You can spend all day dealing with these monkeys and you could have, as a consequence, a well-run school. You will be managing the day-to-day concerns of the institution and, in so doing, driving yourself into the ground. But you won't be doing your job. Of course, you must ensure that the school is well managed. You are driving the galley slaves. But you have to provide leadership. And you can't provide vision, innovation and the promotion of achievement if you are reactive. You need to set the agenda, not service the agenda of others. And make no mistake, teachers will be happy for you to do this. They like the idea that they can hand their issues on to others. Of course, you will want to support your colleagues in any way you can but you mustn't be abused by them. You are master, not slave.

5 Your reputation

They'll be watching you

The way you are perceived as a deputy will largely be based upon one thing – your performance as a classroom teacher. You may feel that this is, to some extent, rather unfair. After all, on your appointment you may have believed that you were leaving all that behind. But you are not. Even more so than the head, you will be judged by teachers on what they believe you can do in the classroom. This is how they measure everyone – by their performance in the job that they do themselves. No matter how knowledgeable or professional they may be, outside speakers and INSET facilitators will find their reception based upon how they appear to measure up in some sort of fantasy situation. Could they deal with the school's notoriously stroppy Year 9 class? They may no longer have to do this. It may not be relevant to their delivery on establishing coherent assessment procedures. But this doesn't matter. Teachers will mutter over their coffee and biscuits. What can they tell me? When were they last in the classroom? It is obviously unfair, but such hostility and cynicism is a staffroom requirement in the profession it seems. Well, you will also be measured in the same way.

The difference is that you will be in the school all the time. The way teachers judge each other never varies. And you will be teaching. A non-teaching deputy is an unusual breed indeed. In fact, virtually all deputies would reject such a concept. You are not ready to abandon the classroom entirely. So classroom performance is one thing that you have to get right. Whatever you bring to the school in terms of vision and insight, you have to bring classroom excellence. Without this you are nothing.

Your colleagues will be keen to learn that the person who has been promoted above them can actually do the business. And perhaps equally keen to catch you out. You must make sure that your lessons are well-planned and organized. Your marking needs to be up-to-date and accurate. It stands to reason that if you are to offer guidance and support, if you are going to offer meaningful performance-management processes, you have to indicate that you are in a strong position to give advice. If that notorious Year 9 class are happy to rip the whiteboard from the wall in the middle of your geography lesson, you are hardly best placed to discuss underperformance with a young French teacher who finds it difficult to get homework from them. Word gets around in a small community like a school very quickly. Everyone will know. Everyone is ready to pass judgement. They will expect you to get things right from the first moment you walk through the door. There is certainly no supportive settling-in period for you, as far as the staff are concerned anyway. So if Nadia swears at you and you do nothing, then the entire school will know before it is time to go home. Don't be at all paranoid, just remember that everyone is watching you all the time. Do the business as well as you always have or your credibility will be shot to pieces and you will find that your career is built on shifting sands.

Get to your lessons on time; ensure order and purpose. On the other hand, you don't want to become the unapproachable ogre with no sense of balance or compassion. That is a particularly hard act to sustain anyway if it doesn't come naturally to you. Be professional. Be the sort of teacher you want the staff in your school to be, the sort of teacher you would want to teach your own children. It is essential that you lead by example. Of course it is hard. It requires energy and commitment and the ability to juggle different priorities successfully. But if you can't do this then you shouldn't think of becoming a deputy.

Another way in which you will be judged is by the way in which you speak to your colleagues. They'll be watching you. They will expect a calm and assured performance from you, not mumbling and nervous incoherence. Talk rubbish in a disjointed way, make sarcastic comments without understanding the politics of your new school or make weak jokes that expire upon the staffroom carpet and you will be a talking point for the rest of the day. This is something that you need to master –

and quickly. In both your daily performances when you have to tell teachers who is away and who was excluded yesterday, and in your presentations when you outline policy, you need to show confidence. You need to give the impression that you are in control, for you need to take your colleagues with you, as an assured and informed leader. Don't let any message seep out to a few staff at a time. If you have an important message to give, speak to the staff formally and all at the same time. It adds a professional sense of formality and occasion to what you say. It is not about creating a sense of mystery, it confirms the dignity of the position that you hold. Also, you do not want to give the impression that you have favourites to whom you reveal little nuggets of information prior to a meeting.

Explain things carefully, in a logical and planned way. It is better to speak from prepared notes if it ensures that you don't miss anything out. Use technology to help with the message as long as you handle it confidently. You don't want to look foolish in front of a PowerPoint presentation when you are telling staff they have got to be more up-to-date in their outlook.

When it comes to explaining a decision you have made, give plenty of background – why you arrived at a decision, what forces were acting upon you, what your intentions are, what the outcomes will be, how you will determine success. Teachers will accept your decisions if you present the arguments logically.

Explain how your decision will affect others. This is something they will be interested in, especially if it is going to influence established working practices. Make sure that, by the time you have finished, you have said all the things that you wanted to say. When you have done this, you are then ready to answer questions.

Always give people the chance to question what you do, but don't allow them to force you off the path you have chosen. Because if you do that, you will never achieve anything and your reputation will be undermined. You will merely confirm to others that they are better qualified to do your job, since they are framing your decisions for you. You are a leader and a leader has to make decisions. Seek consensus, but in the end trust your own judgement to force through changes.

If you have to criticize staff, avoid blanket statements in a staff meeting. Teachers hate these general, vague complaints. They are seen as a coward's way out, a means by which you can avoid confronting an individual. It is particularly galling if staff are being told off for being late to afternoon registration if you are one of those who is always there on time. Confront the individual. At least they can be under no misapprehension that you are talking about them! It is not always as difficult as it first might appear. It is all in the choice of words. 'I can't help noticing . . . Do you need any help in . . . I'll tell you what we can do . . .. Have you noticed how unsettled your class are when . . .' They will know what you mean. As long as you achieve the effect that you seek and you have perhaps preserved the dignity of the person you are talking to, then you have succeeded. But always be ready to confront someone directly if you have to. You can do this if you have established your own reputation as a quality performer in the classroom. That is what you are paid to do.

6 Your teaching

Teach your children well

From the moment you are appointed as deputy head teaching is no longer the simple and uncomplicated activity you may have thought it was. You will suddenly become aware of the host of expectations that other people will have of you. Obviously you don't become a bad teacher overnight. You don't suddenly become a teacher who can only deal with the disaffected. Yet you may suddenly find yourself amongst others who believe that this has become your destiny. Let's be frank, in many cases, what staffroom colleagues want is nothing more than someone who can scare the pants off Year 9 with merely a glance.

In fact, you reached this point in your career because you were recognized as a person with qualities. We can all show talents and abilities in different ways. Always keep hold of that idea. You don't have to fit into everyone's ideas of what a deputy head should be. You don't have to be the enforcer with the loud voice. You may not have been appointed because of your fearful presence, but rather on the basis of your intellect and imagination. Dealing with difficult students may not be your strength. Why should it be so? It doesn't have to be.

Yet life is never that simple. People might expect you to show these skills because that is what they want, which can be very different from what the school needs. A head of department has a difficult class to unload and suddenly you are expected to teach them. Many teachers haven't got much of a perspective beyond themselves and find it hard to imagine that your job might in some way be fundamentally different to theirs. They think it should be exactly the same, but with additional grief. As a result, it might appear sometimes that you should be punished for being promoted. If you don't handle a dodgy class successfully, it could have serious consequences for your school. You are suddenly responsible for a little pocket of chaos and in your position poor performance is unacceptable.

It is not just teachers who have expectations of you. Make no mistake about it. You could be targeted specifically by the more thinking villains. They will see you as a means of revenge, as a way of striking back against the machine that enslaves them. You could be in for a rough ride.

Why shouldn't you have discipline problems? Just because you are deputy head doesn't change the fact that, at times, managing young people can be exceedingly difficult. They respect neither position nor reputation. So why should you take all the difficult classes? Why should teachers automatically assume that you can?

If you do and it goes pear-shaped, then suddenly the smell of disorder will spread through the student body. This will have serious consequences for the school. A senior member of staff run ragged by a class? Where does that leave everyone else? What do you do? Call for assistance from a teacher who is likely to be paid less than you are? Or try and ignore it? Except you can't. The jungle drums will beat out an unmistakable message. This deputy head is fair game. If you are then called to deal with an issue in someone else's classroom, both you and the poor teacher will be undermined if you can't deal with it convincingly. Suddenly that little pocket of chaos is expanding. You don't need this. The school doesn't need this. If going nose-to-nose with the disaffected is not your specialism then it is better you stay out of the firing line. It might not go down well with your colleagues but it may be better for the school. In fact, the whole issue is fraught with dilemmas. It is, like so many other things in school, defined by complex politics. You are leading teachers and some of them may not be happy at all about being led, and you will be leading students, some of whom will want to test you out as well.

In the end, you need to be true to yourself, just as much in the classroom as in the staffroom. You mustn't go into your new job believing you are obliged to frighten witless every child you meet because that is what deputies are expected to do. You will need to build a relationship with any class you teach, in the same way that you did before. Remember the qualities that you believe in and are committed to developing in yourself and others. They are not suddenly negotiable just because you are a deputy. Being a good teacher is based upon commitment, accessibility and relationships. This will always be so. You must continue to show these qualities.

To get a dodgy class to work, you need to establish a relationship with them, whether you are deputy head or a supply teacher. But in your position, once you have done this that relationship could be invaluable because the class will tell you all sorts of things that some teachers might not want you to know. You won't have to go fishing for this information. It will be offered to you freely and openly as part of normal classroom dialogue. It can be a real insight into life in the swamp.

Of course it works both ways. If your teaching is, for whatever reason, not up to scratch then word will spread and your position in the staffroom could be undermined. So make sure that your marking is up-to-date, your mark book an example to all and your reports coherent, incisive and delivered on time.

Perhaps in the early days teach, if you can, the things you are comfortable with and in the way that has always worked for you. It gives you a bit of breathing space and helps you establish yourself. Yes, it's demanding but it is essential. Your job is to lead teachers and that includes setting a good example as a classroom teacher. A headteacher may be forced ultimately to withdraw from the classroom. You will never do this. You must be a role model for young teachers and for the students. A tough call, but if you can't accept it then you need to do something else.

You might find yourself in a school in financial difficulties which requires an increased teaching load. Or it may be that in your subject area there is no one with sufficient knowledge or experience who can fulfil particular obligations to the students. But think carefully before making this decision. You have a wider obligation now and the decision may not necessarily be the right one for the school. You are not there to win brownie points from your colleagues through the sort of sacrifice of your interests that can drive you into the ground. The fact remains that if you try to fulfil all expectations then you are likely to fail. As I said earlier, if you are not the fierce unyielding disciplinarian then this is hardly a role you can act. If you try to adopt this role it might not work at all. You will be more convincing if you are natural. You were appointed because of who you are and what you have done, so it is important that you remain that person. Your reputation will have travelled before you. The bush telegraph is especially efficient. Of course your classroom style may need to be moderated, but if the mainstay of your teaching style is to be relaxed and approachable, then don't sacrifice this. Before your appointment it made you a success. Never deny it.

Some subject leaders may feel particularly threatened by your presence, especially if you come from elsewhere. A struggling middle manager may not see you as an asset. And when you see the work of that subject leader, it can be hard to watch them do those things badly that perhaps only weeks before you were doing so well. You will want to offer support and guidance and you will not want to undermine, but you do have that fundamental responsibility to the students in the school. You cannot condone failure merely because you don't want to upset a teacher. If you see things going badly wrong, then you can always suggest flexible timetable arrangements whereby you teach particular modules or sections to classes. It is a good staff-development opportunity that shouldn't be ignored. Invite them to observe your lessons; do a bit of team-teaching. Show that you have something positive to offer.

On the other hand, you might suddenly find yourself in a highly successful department which may be ready to test you out. Either way, remember the skills that brought you to your new post. You didn't get the job because you were average. You were good. You are good.

And if you are not happy with the role that is being allocated to you because it isn't exploiting your strengths, then do not accept it. It may not be popular. It may not be your style. But sometimes for the good of the school, as you see it, you might have to pull rank.

7 Relationships with teachers

Learn to love them

What you will soon notice, if you were not aware of this before, is that the term 'senior management' has become a pejorative term. It is often said with a sneer, with contempt. It carries the suggestion that the head and their cronies haven't a clue about what is going on. Only the speaker (and their cronies) knows the fearsome reality of life in the swamp.

When you become a deputy you cross a dividing line that takes you away, probably forever, from a cosy little grumble with a break-time cup of coffee. Your role now straddles the invisible line that delineates 'senior management', the crossing of which, according to some, suddenly turns you into a wildly incompetent teacher with neither technique nor philosophy. But never forget where your professional loyalties now lie. People's expectations of you will be much greater because you will be operating in front of a bigger audience. Whereas before those you were managing may have been united by the common experience of a curriculum area or a responsibility, now you are leading the whole staff.

It may be that you had a difficult staffing issue to deal with in your previous post and have gained lots of painful experience. On the other hand, everything may have been vibrant and everyone supportive, a happy collective of excellence. In either case don't assume that all relationships will be the same. Be prepared. At some point you will certainly have to confront, perhaps for the first time in your career, opposition and hostility. Don't take this to heart. Remain confident in your vision. Listen to what others say but stick with your principles. This is why you were appointed.

Remember, teachers are resistant to change. Examine carefully what you believe to be the motives of those who express unhappiness with your plans. Are they motivated by a genuine concern for the well-being and progress of the students? Do they have an alternative or a variant they are prepared to discuss? Is their agenda different from yours? Or are they merely quirky? A vocal member of staff may be doing nothing more than cementing their position with their colleagues as unofficial leader of the opposition, with a mission to oppose and obstruct everything that the leadership team proposes. In these circumstances you must be confident in you own ability and position. Their opposition to your ideas doesn't mean they can't teach and should be ignored. Neither does it mean that you are wrong. It could all be part of the arcane politics of the staffroom. Perhaps it is all about them and not at all about you. And if you had spent 22 years in the battered chair to the left of the kettle you'd say no to everything too, especially if the head of mathematics is in favour . . . Just be thankful that you don't need to be involved. Just remember – and don't be afraid to remind them now and again – that their prime responsibility, like yours, is to teach properly and successfully. School is no more complicated than that.

It is strange, almost contradictory. Teachers are often anti-authoritarian figures. They spend their time trying to achieve control in the classroom, using their authority to lead and direct their students. But they hate being told what to do themselves. If you can find the time, it is fascinating to observe this peculiar phenomenon. There is always the cynic who has seen it all and it is foolish to think that you can win everyone round. Of course you can't. You have to lead and direct and in the end the teachers don't have to like you. They don't have to agree with you. They must discharge their responsibilities to their students within the context that you have been appointed to create. They will see your professionalism and your sense of duty, but they may choose not to recognize or acknowledge it. Never forget that many teachers believe they can do your job better than you. It is only that they haven't been given the opportunity. Don't worry about that. Remember, if you do the job well it will look easy. Anyone can do it. If you don't do it well – and after reading this book there is obviously no chance of that – then they will say that they can do it better. So never think that you can win. At the same time also remember that being quirky or difficult does not preclude anyone from being an exceptional teacher. In the end that is what you must learn to value; talent in the classroom. You can put up with the rest. Let them be difficult but never let them be destructive.

When you present your decisions be logical but be prepared to be insistent if you have to be. Through your appointment you have won the right to take these decisions. There is a good reason why you are paid more than them. If they are so keen to set the agenda for a school, then they should develop their own career in the same way that you have developed yours.

Teachers are full of opinions. It is their job to have them, to construct arguments, to discuss issues. In many cases it is the life blood of their subject. As a result they will have an opinion about everything that you do. And usually a contrary one. They may feel that any idea they have is exactly what the school needs. Be prepared to listen, but to say no, unambiguously, based upon your position and experience. You are under no obligation to act. You now have a perspective that they might not have acquired. Their comments may merely reflect a genetic pre-disposition to contradict anything anyone else says. By some secret process as old as time itself, the possession of this quality singled them out for a career in teaching.

Always retain a perspective. Not all teachers are exceptional. Not all teachers are dreadful. Don't get yourself into a state of mind where you believe that they have nothing to offer but merely complaints and opposition. Be ready to use the expertise of your staff. As a collective they will know far more than you can ever hope to know – certainly about their own subjects. They might also know about past students or siblings or parents, which could prove to be valuable information.

Show a concern for the professional development of your colleagues. You wouldn't be in post if someone hadn't shown you similar support and encouragement. Never assume that not one of them is capable of doing your job.

And always remember that, like you, they have complex personal lives to organize and manage. As a sensitive manager you will be ready to accommodate their personal needs – for doctor's appointments or sick children. It is part of working in a supportive community. But don't forget that you have these rights too. Never deny yourself the flexibility with which you treat your colleagues. What's more important anyway? Your family? Or the English department? I hope that this is not too difficult a question for you to answer.

8 Working with your staff

Be positive

As a leader you will see the effect you have on your school in many ways. But perhaps the most significant way you influence the school is in the ways that you can't see. Through your actions and your presence you create a tone and this has far-reaching consequences. This will be displayed in both your relationships with students and with teachers and other staff.

You will want to establish a community that is confident, professional and cooperative. These are the values you will want to promote. If you manage it, you will exclude far fewer students than a school with a similar profile that is cynical, fearful and introverted. Others will take a lead from you. So create an ethos and a management style that makes your school a happy place. Hold doors open yourself and students will soon copy you. Learn their names, greet them in the morning, set the tone. Be positive in assembly and in the staffroom.

Remember how important praise can be, especially when it comes from someone with seniority. That praise should not be confined to the students. Recognize what your colleagues achieve and don't be embarrassed about celebrating their achievements. You are now a living example of the successful professional. You might not feel that way but you are. Younger colleagues may be unable to imagine themselves doing your job or showing the sort of confidence you display. Of course, one day they will. You have to show that professional standards are important and apply to everyone. For example, as far as reports are concerned, make sure they can be used as exemplars. Set the kind of targets for students that you expect from others and deliver them on time. Your performance is always under the microscope. This is just one example of how you lead your staff and it shows how you are always different things to different people. You are the jovial dispenser of *bonhomie* on prize day. You are the enforcer in the yard, the expert in the classroom, the respected professional at parents' evening, the relaxed and informed leader in the staffroom. You will spend many days juggling these different hats. After a while you will come to realize that relationships with students are easy to control. The parameters are fixed. The dynamics are clear. But with staff it is always less clear cut.

Where you might experience some problems is, in fact, that some staff feel that what you say applies to everyone else except themselves. So there will be occasions when you will have to speak to staff directly. There is no point in dressing things up and making vague comments about poor timekeeping. It is better in the end to be specific and pointed when necessary. 'Ah yes. Mr Brown. I can't help noticing . . . ' 'Could I offer you some advice . . . ' 'I'd like to support you since we are trying to . . . ' 'As you know one of our targets is . . . '

It is not unusual for staff to believe that the words 'leadership and management' only apply to you. As classroom teachers they have no truck with such things. Nonsense, of course. Everyone in any position of responsibility in school has to lead a team of other people and to manage resources. Every teacher must manage their own classroom and the students in it. It is easy for them to say that leadership isn't their responsibility. But it is and anyone making judgements on the success of leadership within the school will be considering all staff and the way they make their decisions. The key question is how effective they are in doing it.

Some heads of department − thankfully fewer than there used to be − approach leadership with all the confidence of a fish up a tree. They may have been appointed on the basis of their subject knowledge or even longevity, not on their ability to lead. This can often prove extremely frustrating for younger members of a department. You have to show that you support the head of department, whilst at the same time ensuring that the development of younger teachers is not stifled. It is a hard one to balance. But remember, throwing more INSET at old Frankie, the head of art, may not be the answer. If it hasn't worked so far then what guarantee do you have that it will work now? Perhaps the best answer is to concentrate more upon succession planning and prepare Sara, your bright young art teacher, for promotion either in your school or elsewhere.

You must remember that you were appointed to make decisions, not merely to action a consensus reached by the staff. However, that is no licence to become an inflexible autocrat. It is always a good idea to gather together the staff perceptions and priorities to help inform policy and development planning. Don't just consult the teachers either. Other staff will have equally valid and informed contributions to make. You don't have a monopoly on good ideas. But don't be too eager to please everyone. You must not find yourself implementing changes that you know are wrong. Staffrooms change as they develop and as the inhabitants change, and a staffroom can reach a point where their agenda reveals an eroded sense of professionalism. Changes suggested to the school might be designed to make their own lives better. In surveys of what makes a good school, teachers generally rank first issues like staff development and communication and involvement, along with comments about a pleasant environment in which to work. Of course these things are important. You would not deny it for a moment. But the most important thing in a school has to be the quality of the teaching experience. The teachers are not doing the students a favour by coming to school. The school is doing the teachers a favour. It is paying them. So listen to them, assess what they say, but back your own judgement.

If you make a mistake, though, admit it. If your idea isn't working then stop. If your plan has been sabotaged then that is a different matter altogether, but, as the Cherokee proverb has it, 'If the horse is dead the best thing you can do is to get off.' It is not a weakness to say that you got something wrong, it is your responsibility to do so. Don't drag your school into a wasteland, justifying the illogical and the wrong. There are bigger issues at stake than your pride. Some staff will respect you more for this, others less. But you can't allow yourself to be troubled by this. You must back your judgement but always measure it with the most rigorous of tests. Then act upon the conclusions. In the end you can't please every member of your staff. You can't suddenly become the distant figure of authority who can quell a major riot with a glance if it isn't your style. If that was what the school wanted then they wouldn't have appointed you. You have different strengths.

One strength you must have, however, is the ability to deal with your staff and one of the first things you must do on appointment is to get to know them. Obviously you shouldn't go around asking awkward questions in an insensitive way, but remember the things you are told. The longer you are there and the more comfortable staff become with you, and you thus gain their respect, the more you will find out. And you need to find out lots about them. Their backgrounds. The things they bring with them to school every day. All these little details make them a person. They are not irrelevant. They are part of the person who you employ and if you are to show them a duty of care as a sensitive employer, you need to have a picture of the wider self.

The autistic son

The handicapped mother

The volatile marriage

The irritable bowel

Difficult teenagers

Ageing parents

The list is almost endless, but you cannot deal with your staff separately from the things that make them what they are. And it is not gossip. Learning such information can be extremely important on social occasions for example. If someone is gay you need to be aware so that you can monitor and address discrimination issues. A member of a religious group or faith may have particular requirements, for example with regard to dietary requirements. For the staff social committee to choose a venue which effectively excludes someone because it doesn't accommodate such needs could be seen as discriminatory. You need to know such things.

You have a duty of care and you'd want to carry out that duty for ethical reasons anyway but it also makes good employment sense. Staff who are made to feel unhappy by perceived discrimination will be less productive and demotivated. At the very least they might resign, bringing consequent recruitment and training costs to the school, as well as damaging your reputation. If you breach your duty of care, then you might be regarded as negligent. So you have to keep your wits about you.

It is also important that you remember that all social occasions are potentially dangerous. Never forget that your position has changed and now has a political dimension. However much you try, you can't be one of the gang again. This is especially the case if you have been appointed from within the school. It will be on a social occasion that you will be aware of how much your position has changed, because now this is not a social occasion at all. You are on duty. People will remember what you do. They will remember what you say. Others will try to extract state secrets from you – and a careless word at the bar or an injudicious comment that penetrates the noise of the disco could come back to haunt you. When you become a manager you become a focal point in the fetid world of staffroom politics. Always remember who and what you are and what others might want from you. You are permitted to regret the changes that time and age have brought. Yes, you were once part of a staffroom outing that put the art teacher in a skip on the high street, but no longer. And if you find that difficult to accept, then this is the wrong job for you.

9 Saying no

There is a skill to saying no and it is one that you need to learn very quickly. It is not your job to be the deputy that the staff want you to be. You must be the deputy the governors want and the school needs. These may not necessarily be the same thing. Here is a cynical view of the staffroom. It is a place where you will find teachers who just want an easy life. The fact that they are not doing your job may be because they lost sight of their professional obligations some time ago and exchanged their vocation for a comfy chair in the staffroom and a reluctance to accept change. Deputies come and deputies go and what they need to ensure is that as little changes as possible and that you do as much of their work for them as is possible. And they might be full of ideas to make sure this happens.

Of course, I have overstated the case but it is certainly true that some will try to define your role for you. They want you to respond to their needs, to sort out their problems. You must find them more money, shout at their classes, take difficult children from them, cover for absence, do all the jobs round the school that they don't fancy. And you can all too easily fall into this trap. But it is not what your job should be. You should be dealing with priorities, strategic direction, articulating a vision. And in order to do this most of the time you will need to say no. You can't expect to be Father Christmas, delivering presents and favours with a hearty chuckle. Teachers' needs should be part of the development plan that is putting into practice the aspirations of the school. As a result there will be those who will be disappointed.

Try to avoid making decisions to meet someone else's agenda and before you are properly prepared. 'What you have to say is very interesting. Perhaps you can come to my office to discuss it.' Give them a time when you can meet in the next day or so. In the interim you can do your research. You can discuss it with other senior colleagues if you have to. Plan out what you are going to say. Then whip out the hospitality tray and hold your meeting. Begin by asking them to present their request or case. Then work through your points logically to the conclusion that you want. Always refer back to the school's strategic plan. Indicate that what they have to say is interesting, but that it is not currently one of the school's priorities, if indeed it isn't. This is particularly useful if they hadn't included their request in their original development plan for their department, for example. You can say that, of course, current priorities will be reviewed and that it could be incorporated at a later stage once it has been properly planned and budgeted. But if it is an especially madcap idea you will have to say that at the moment you do not feel that the school can support it You might need to explain that, whilst theirs is an interesting idea, the school is working within a restricted budget. Mind you, as an argument, the financial one rings hollow after a while.

You must treat your staff as adults, even when they are being brainless. Avoid pulling rank if you can. This emphasizes the difference between you and them. Once you are a deputy your perspective must be broader and impartial. You need to look beyond subject boundaries. Your staff will themselves hold important parts of the jigsaw but you have the picture on the box that shows where all the pieces go.

10 Stress

Is it stress? Is it anxiety? Is it tension? Is it always a bad thing?

We hear a lot about stress in school. Some teachers talk about it all the time. And undoubtedly it is a stressful job. Dealing with a difficult class that you are expected to lead to examination success can be bad enough. But if you are facing an inspection or you are working in a failing department, or you are snowed under by paperwork that you despise, you might well feel that you are experiencing stress. Perhaps you are. But stress and tension are not always bad things. For some they are creative forces. They might just give you the focus to get things done. They might indeed be a necessary motivational drive.

Let's face it, you achieved promotion by showing that you can deal with situations that others may find stressful. You developed strategies for dealing with the situations or for dealing with the pressure. Others may not be able to develop these attitudes. So don't always try to judge staff by your own successful standards or attributes. Everyone is different and not everyone has the capacity to deal with pressure and tension in a successful way. However, you are in a position naturally to offer advice about how stress can be managed. Your job is stressful too, so share with them how you deal with it. Go home early one night, you know you want too. Don't neglect your family, don't neglect the things you enjoy, share the pleasures and the pain of the classroom with your colleagues, keep a perspective, take exercise – you know the strategies yourself.

It must, of course, become a genuine concern of yours that you are not, through your decisions, creating a climate in which stress grows.

You do not want to be responsible for decisions that make the conditions of your colleagues worse than they are. But neither do you want only to make popular decisions. What you want to do is to make the right decisions. And when you do so, then some will always complain that you have not solved a problem but created one. You will undoubtedly meet staff who claim that their stress is your fault. Often they are talking rubbish. All you have done is to challenge accepted practice that in your judgement was wrong. Those who claim the symptoms of stress so casually, detract unnecessarily from those who are genuinely being made ill by the pressures of work. In your position you are vulnerable to such accusations. It is part of decision-making. Do something unpopular, something that changes someone's comfortable working practices or shakes them out of complacency and you might find yourself accused. Don't immediately worry about this. Many staff threaten you with their stress as a means of indicating that you are not doing your job properly and as a way of getting back at you. If it happens, just step back and consider what you have done. If your decision was, in your judgement, the right thing for the school and thus benefited the students, then stick by it. It is what you are paid for.

The assumption has to be that a member of staff can withstand the normal pressures of the job. It is a job that they signed up to do. If they don't like being in the classroom and claim that it's causing stress, then they haven't got much of a case. Kids in classrooms can't be much of a surprise. If it causes anxiety then perhaps there needs to be some reflection about whether this was the wisest of career choices. You can't take responsibility for this. 'I am sorry that you find lesson observations so stressful, but I am afraid that they are now a normal part of the job . . . '

Where stress becomes an issue is if it is the cause of psychiatric illness. It is at such a point that industrial tribunals start to beckon. 'Could this illness have been foreseen or prevented if the leadership team had acted differently?' You need to consider this question. Have you deliberately added to someone else's stress through an ill-conceived decision? But consider it, too, alongside a consideration of whether previous practice was acceptable. If you change the time-honoured policy of the head of French taking the top classes, even though someone else is much better equipped, then this is a change that might cause stress but which has been made for professionally supportable reasons. You will have foreseen that this might cause a problem and you have therefore prepared for it by offering support and training. Remember, you have not been appointed to become popular. You are acting in the best interests of the students. You can't allow consideration for teachers to replace your obligations to the student body.

Where you could be in difficulties would be if a member of staff alerted you to their problem and you ignored it. In this case if you did nothing to help the head of French develop the skills needed to teach more challenging groups. If you are told about it, do something, because when they tell you then you are officially sharing the problem. You can't ignore it. That is neglect and that is unprofessional.

The challenge then is to deal with the case without making some other teacher's workload unmanageable. All you will be doing then is shifting an issue from one teacher to another. So you might initially consider re-allocating duties when complaints about stress and workload issues land on your desk. However, perhaps a more effective option is to look at the way someone works. What can you do to reduce or change their workload? Do they need help in planning and prioritizing? Are they finding it difficult to delegate, for whatever reason? Are their skills no longer appropriate? Then you must ask yourself, what can I do to stop the condition deteriorating?

You can employ a supply teacher for a short period to support your member of staff, allowing them to work on a part-time basis for a while. Much depends upon the school's financial circumstances because it is an expensive thing to do, but it might be better, and ultimately cheaper, than losing a colleague permanently through psychiatric illness.

You need to be proactive in dealing with your staff. This where it is really important to know your staff and why you need to establish honest and open relationships. If you are made aware of a situation in someone's life that makes them vulnerable, like a divorce or bereavement, then it would be wrong to ignore it. But remember, you are not a doctor. You have to take what you are told about someone's well-being as the truth, unless you have a very good reason to think to the contrary. You should not make searching enquiries because you are not sufficiently qualified to contradict professional advice, and scepticism, based upon nothing more than instinct, may cause additional harm. It is for others to pass judgement on medical conditions. You must act properly in the best interests of your school – and that encompasses the members of staff and the students that they teach.

11 Staff grievances

Learn the procedures

There is a huge reservoir of talent in the teaching profession. You will meet some of the most talented people in your life in the staffroom. Creative, original thinkers, skilled artisans, talented communicators. But it is also true to say that you will meet some of the oddest. It is one of the mental shifts that you will have to make when you become a deputy, the shift to adopting a whole-school perspective that results, inevitably, in your perceptions of staff changing. You are not one of them anymore. You will see them differently. Their idiosyncrasies will now be something that you must manage.

Let's face it, teachers are a strange bunch. Argumentative. Inflexible. Used to getting their own way. It is for this reason that you need to familiarize yourself with staff grievance procedures. It is highly likely that disagreements amongst the staff themselves and between the teaching staff and members of the leadership team will result at some point in a grievance.

Any employee can have a concern that they wish to raise. The grievance process exists to provide a mechanism to deal with issues in a structured way before they develop into major problems. The issues that can lead to a grievance include terms and conditions of employment, health and safety, bullying and harassment, and equal opportunities. In October 2004 statutory grievance procedures became law, providing a minimum process that employer and employees must follow. You should try and foster the sort of environment in school that minimizes the possibility that grievances might occur. Always consult staff about major changes you might make and encourage staff to raise concerns informally as soon as they arise. Given the nature of teachers, you might consider this to be a vain hope!

You will need to make sure that your grievance procedure is inclusive and that it makes it easy for staff to raise issues with the leadership team. The process should be simple, and allow for confidentiality. You must also check on the current status of legislation. At the time of writing the standard statutory grievance procedure has three distinct phases:

- The first step is for the employee to forward a written complaint to the employer.
- The second stage requires the employer to invite the employee to a hearing at which the alleged grievance can be discussed. Then, after the meeting, the employer must inform the employee of any decision and offer them the right of appeal.
- If the member of staff still believes that their grievance has not been resolved then they must inform the employer that they intend to make an appeal against the decision or failure to make a decision. This is the third stage.

A more senior manager should attend the appeal hearing, after which the employer must communicate its final decision to the employee.

It is a simple, easily understood procedure. Staff are allowed to be accompanied by a companion who can lend support during a difficult and anxious period. As far as you are concerned the process can be less draining if you also have support. Ensure that there is someone there to take notes and to compile a detailed written record. You never know when it might be needed.

This is the basic process. Your own governors or LEA may have a policy that varies from this so you must make sure that you know how it is meant to operate. Don't regard it as a failure on your part if the grievance procedure has to be used. It is almost inevitable that it will appear soon enough. Consider it as a way of making sure that minor disagreements do not escalate into big problems.

12 Staff discipline

Preserve the integrity of our profession

This is sadly an important area. It isn't important because you will be dealing with it every day. It is important because of the difficulties you might find yourself in if you get it wrong. This is obvious, I suppose. You might be dealing with someone's career and lifestyle so you must be absolutely certain that everything is right and proper. It is hard to have to accept that others who have followed the same profession as yourself do not share your commitment. Having to speak to a teacher on issues of discipline can be very difficult. What you will need to do in the first place is to take advice. This is essential. You will only be able to pick your way through the minefield of your legal obligations if you seek help at an early stage. Get it wrong early on, and it will all backfire on you very suddenly.

You can turn to your LEA and to your professional association. You should also keep yourself up-to-date by subscribing to journals that specialize in education law. This is never money wasted. They might also run conferences too. The key idea is to stay informed in a fast-changing area. Any specific advice offered here would quickly become out of date. Just remember never to neglect your obligation to stay informed of changes to employment law or to child protection.

Your school will have a policy on disciplinary issues and staff have a right to know about it. The adoption of standard disciplinary procedures became statutory in October 2004. Any policy must include an awareness of what staff can do if they want to appeal against a decision. But the most important thing isn't an exemplary set of procedures. It is how they are implemented that matters.

It always helps to deal with problems quickly, and obviously many disciplinary matters are dealt with informally. You will almost certainly have to be involved in this at some time or another. It comes with the territory.

You must remember, however, that you are restricted to issuing a verbal warning for any misdemeanour. There can be no such thing as a written informal warning. That is contradictory. An informal warning cannot be placed on an employee's file. It is just what it says – a reminder to address misconduct or to improve performance that is a cause for concern.

There will be big issues that require a serious response – theft, malicious damage, violence, dishonesty. The governing body can dismiss on a first offence if it is serious enough. Other issues like poor time-keeping or unauthorized absence will be dealt with differently. You will need to familiarize yourself with the details of current policy as a priority. But don't hide behind a policy. Don't avoid taking an issue or an individual on just because it is difficult. If you need to speak to someone then do it. Be firm, clear and absolutely sure of the facts. Remain measured. If appropriate, set targets for improvement.

> 'I have noticed that you are frequently late for school. The traffic can be so difficult these days. What I would like you to do is to sign in at the school office when you arrive. Let's see if we can establish a helpful pattern. It must be really difficult rushing into registration every day without a chance to prepare for it. This should help you to plan your journey. Let's try it for a couple of weeks. See how we get on shall we?'

Naturally any action you take needs to be proportionate. But whatever you say, monitor it closely and note signs of improvement. This will make you feel better because you will feel that what you did was worthwhile. If that doesn't work then you will need to remind them once more of their professional obligations and indicate that this might lead to formal proceedings on the basis of their failure to attend the morning briefing in the staffroom. Of course, you need to document everything. An accurate record of problems perceived and remedial action taken is essential.

Dealing with such issues properly will enable minor issues to be handled without disrupting the core purpose of your school. These things happen because the school is full of people who behave as people do, being forgetful, making mistakes. Rarely is it malicious. But it can happen.

Once you get into the area of formal warnings then you must tread carefully. This is by no means to say that you should avoid formal procedures completely. In fact your professional duty may impose upon you an obligation to take action. Just make sure you do it properly – and always take advice.

The first stage is always going to be the collection of evidence to determine whether or not disciplinary action is appropriate. It is quite likely that the deputy may be asked to do this, though it could be any member of the leadership team. You would need to look at documents or consult witnesses. This may require you to question students. It is always a good idea to write down what any witnesses say as a statement and then ask them to sign it and date it.

Once you have sufficient information you may decide that you really do need to call a disciplinary meeting. Obviously the member of staff must know what the problem is and be given an opportunity to answer it. The employee must have written notice of a hearing a reasonable time in advance. This letter should make very clear the nature of the meeting. You can't leave any doubt in anyone's mind that this is disciplinary and that there could be consequences. It should be issued in sufficient time for the employee to gather evidence with which to defend themselves and to organize a colleague or union official to accompany them.

Once the meeting has been fixed then arrange for someone to attend to write full notes of the meeting. You don't want to be distracted by the need to take notes and you certainly don't want to rely upon someone else's transcript of events.

After the hearing, it is possible that an employee may receive a warning or indeed may be dismissed. Dismissal can follow a case of gross misconduct even if it is a first offence. For example, in the event of the art teacher assaulting the headteacher. Dismissal may also be appropriate if further offences have happened during the life of a previous warning (either 6 or 12 months).

If the complaint is dismissed then confirm this in writing. If the governing body is satisfied that the hearing was fair and that dismissal is justified, the employee should be informed in writing of the date of the termination of their contract and of how they can appeal against the decision.

We all hope that the details of this procedure remain theoretical. You would rather go through your school career without having to witness the huge drain on the resources of a school that such procedures can have. But the procedure has to be there, to protect the school, its students and to preserve the integrity of an important profession. As far as you are concerned, if you have any doubts at all about anything take advice. You are a teacher, not a lawyer. If a particular situation threatens to get out of hand where, for example, one member of staff makes allegations against another, then call the police. Better a preventative phone call than that full-blown assault on the headteacher. Or even worse, the deputy.

13 Your relationship with the headteacher

A sparkling fountain of innovation

Not withstanding the fact that, on mature reflection, you would much prefer the head to be hit rather than yourself, your most important professional relationship must always be with the headteacher.

You are not after their job. You are there to help them with theirs. That was why you were appointed. You may have long-term ambitions to be a head and, indeed, your governing body might regard you as a natural successor. But your primary function is to be an integral part of the team that is running the school. That team needs to share ideas, schemes, plans, complaints and the members of it need to feel confident that they can make mistakes without prejudice. If that climate isn't created then no one will take risks, and without risks there may not be effective change.

You need to be able to talk openly and honestly and not feel threatened by disagreement. If you are not confident enough to offer madcap ideas then the leadership team will not thrive. If relationships break down, then the school will suffer. It may even fracture. Disagreement is normal, healthy and promotes thought and reflection. But you must always present a united front. Some staff might be very keen to see and exploit any perceived gaps. There will be those who have little else to do, other than to pick over in minute detail their impressions of power shifts and the politics of the leadership team. It is quite sad really. It is only a school after all.

You must work as a team. You don't have to like each other, though it might help. But you have to share a vision and a desire for success.

It means meeting regularly, both formally and informally. You may not wish to share things socially, but you must share tasks and ideas.

The head will need to examine your performance regularly as part of the cycle. They will set you targets, for both your classroom work and your whole-school duties. Work together on this, because those conversations will shape the future of the school. Your targets will have a much wider impact than most and, in order to achieve them, you may draw upon the resources of others. In this way, together, you should be the intellectual heart of the school. The school needs a sparkling fountain of innovation at the top, not the dead weight of oppressive rejection. This is another of your responsibilities. You and your headteacher need to create this atmosphere and, in doing so, you will be setting the tone for the school and laying the foundations for success.

You have to act as a filter to the head too. Heads like to talk about having an open-door policy, ready to see anyone at anytime. But that isn't always possible. And anyway, do they really need to be dealing with trivia? I don't think so. You need to stop it happening. In fact, it is no bad thing in terms of the overall management of a secondary school if the head is a little aloof, rather than an instantly accessible figure. Available, yes. But not always instantly available.

Your job is firmly rooted in the realities of school life and your practical perspective will be important in informing any decisions that are taken. Your head may feel that it is very important to continue teaching, leading staff from the front. You might feel, however, that the inevitable occasions when the head is called to meetings and thus misses a lesson are unacceptable. It does the head's reputation no good at all if they repeatedly miss a lesson that a colleague must then cover, particularly if that class is a difficult one. And does the head really need the marking and the reports and the preparation? Is this really a valuable use of their time? It is up to you to tell them. They might lead the school, but you manage it and the head must respect this.

To realize how important this relationship can be, perhaps you need to consider what can happen in extreme situations. Just imagine how debilitating it must be for a head to have to deal with the under-performance of a deputy. It happens. A deputy – not you, obviously – can be stuck in a school, all passion spent, washed up and washed out. Or a poor appointment is made – again, not you. A governing body, inexplicably seduced by an expensive suit and a clipboard full of jargon, hangs cheerfully an empty shell on to the bowed shoulders of a harassed head. This can have a terrible effect upon a school. Someone incompetent has seniority. Suddenly the school is drifting towards the rocks. The head has enough to deal with as it is. It is the hardest job in the school. It must be – look at the pay. A deputy is appointed to bring a new perspective and to lend experience and support. If that deputy doesn't have an impact at all then there is no point having one. The head knows that an incompetent deputy can inhibit seriously the performance of the school. This can ruin their own reputation and destroy staff morale.

Of course, there will be performance management procedures. Targets can be set, reviews carried out, training provided. But the reality is that none of this is going to redress the fundamental issues of incompetence. As we are seeing, a deputy requires self-awareness, energy, motivation, a vision. If these virtues are missing can anyone put them there?

I have also seen what happens when a head loses the confidence of his staff and his leadership colleagues through unfortunate illness. Then you have to support and guide. You will want to support the head but never forget that your primary responsibility is to the school and you must do whatever is needed to ensure its success and survival. You might well find yourself taking on ultimate responsibility, whilst you work with the governors and your LEA in order to engineer a dignified exit for the person they once chose to lead the school.

14 Working with the office

Respect. Without them you are nothing

Don't be embarrassed about using the office staff to help you. That is what they are employed to do. For some people it can be an adjustment that is difficult to make. Your career will have been built upon telling children what to do. Now things have changed. Initially you might have some embarrassment at asking adults to do work for you. Of course you shouldn't. They will be expecting you to assume that seniority. They will not question your appointment or your right to ask for some support. You are not employed to carry out clerical tasks. Look again at your salary and try and justify time spent entering data, filing or typing. You can't. You have to make decisions, provide vision and direction. Office staff are there to support you whilst you are doing this. As a result they are extremely important figures and you need to nurture them, because through their efficiency and commitment they can make or break your schemes. Naturally you will always be polite and reasonable. Remember birthdays and Christmas as a way of recognizing the support that they give you.

Something you may have to deal with is that some teachers like to hang around the office. They like to gossip and use the telephone and, in so doing, stop office colleagues from doing their work. They seem to be attracted there because it is a place where their status isn't questioned, not as it is in the classroom. Some – though not all office staff – will need your help to move them on. The best way is to go into the office and give out a piece of work that needs to be done urgently. The teacher will usually leave. If it persists then you will have to ask politely but firmly for them to keep the office clear.

It might be that you will want to restructure roles and responsibilities within the administrative area. As schools change then it is important that elements within the school adapt to reflect those changes. Over time, jobs erode and tasks accrue. So don't let things drift. Change the titles of jobs if you have to, in order to define closely what someone is expected to do. This will also provide the focus. A data manager or attendance officer will have a clear idea of what is expected of them.

Encourage the same professional standards that you would expect of your teaching staff. There should be regular minuted staff meetings with an agenda, there should be training opportunities, job shadowing, career progression and support networks. Office staff are usually the first staff a visitor meets when they arrive in school – and first impressions count. They will deal with all sorts of pupil-related issues like injuries, stroppy parents, local shopkeepers, so their training needs can be varied, from conflict resolution to first aid. Job satisfaction is important, especially since many office staff are completely devoted to the school and have invested a great deal in it throughout many years of service. Don't ever dismiss that. Ask their opinions. They will understand the school just as well as and often better than the teachers.

15 Maintaining a wider perspective

It is your duty to know and to understand

One of the most important parts of your job is keeping yourself fully informed of what is going on in the areas that affect your profession. By so doing you are keeping your school up-to-date and responsive. You should set aside some time every week in the school day in order to maintain your knowledge. Legislation changes so quickly that the school where the deputy is forever in charge of the dinner queue will always be a few paces behind. You have to do it. It might be that your colleagues will grumble if they see you reading in your office or checking out websites, but this is what you have to do. Don't let them define your job for you. You should not be at their beck and call all the time. That is not what your job is about.

This illustrates, should you need to be reminded, that your responsibilities as a deputy are different. You have to show a nimble intellect and the grasp of issues to point the school in a changing direction. Issues from the classroom really are the responsibility of the classroom teacher. You need to be dealing with policy.

Obviously you should check out current guidance. It would be foolish to base any big decisions upon old information. Your best source of information is probably the official websites, especially government ones, and you should check them regularly. You need to read relevant professional publications and in so doing identify material that might be valuable to others and pass it on. Legal issues are particularly relevant and tricky. You need to know not just the law and regulations, but also procedures. These need to be observed meticulously. You will find that subscription to a journal is always worthwhile. This will give you access to advice and invitations to attend conferences. Don't be afraid of taking professional advice from your professional association. That is what you pay your subscription for and they can be contacted easily by phone or on the Internet.

As a deputy you will want to encourage the professional development of your colleagues. You will want the school to be a leader, not a follower. But you must not neglect your own training needs. That is quite easy to do. You will always find pressing management issues that require you to remain in school. And, if you wait for your teaching colleagues to suggest to you that you go on a course or attend a conference, then you will be waiting forever. You must decide these things for yourself. You must take charge of your own professional development and you mustn't let it wither. You wouldn't be the first deputy who felt guilty about going out of school on a course but you shouldn't think that way. There is then but a short step to feeling you are indispensable and this is where madness lies. The teachers in the school are all grown up and can survive without you. If you don't go out on courses, then your own professional development will suffer and you will become someone who only manages the day-to-day events of the school. You won't lead it – and that is what you are paid to do. You can only lead through knowledge and awareness. It will also help you to plug into networks with others, both locally and nationally. It is good to be able to contact colleagues who might have dealt with a similar situation or have materials you can share. Such links could lead to shared INSET opportunities or interesting links at subject level. However, you do not want to be seen as someone who sets up projects and innovation merely for self aggrandizement. There must always be a purpose to such links and connections.

Always remember that the bedrock of all our reputations in school is our performance as a subject teacher. Sometimes it is hard to maintain your subject knowledge but never neglect it. You might need to support a less experienced head of department trying to do the job you once did. Although it can be burdensome, marking for one of the examination boards is an excellent way of maintaining your expertise. You can see what is happening in other schools and it reinforces your own position in the school. That is something you should never dismiss, because it is also showing you as a leader with a sense of responsibility and obligation. All teachers have an obligation to become involved in the examining and assessment procedures that we all share and which measure our students. We can't allow them to become separated from the daily realities of life in the classroom. We all need to understand them and work within them to benefit our schools and candidates. You are no different.

PART TWO

What you have to do

16 Creating the school development plan

You've started but you'll never finish

The most important thing you will do as part of a leadership team is to create the school development plan. Never underestimate the importance of this document. Never despise it as just another piece of paper. It is vital, for it acts as a road map laying out where you want to take the school. Through it you can change fundamentally its shape and priorities. It gives you a planned approach to make changes and ensures that developments are rooted in reality and the implications measured and assessed.

Let us imagine you have decided to put extra money into modern foreign languages and to introduce the study of Portuguese. You think it is important, so you lay out the process in your development plan. You find additional money. You appoint a teacher. You seek out appropriate INSET. You recruit students to this exciting new opportunity. Suddenly you have pushed the school in a new direction.

The plan is a powerful document. You need to build upon what is going well, support areas that need to improve, respond to external pressures like changes to a curriculum or syllabus, support governing body aspirations and articulate your own beliefs.

What is clear is that the leadership team, taking into account all the factors above, needs to set the agenda. Faculties and departments must respond to the framework you set. Of course, there will be specific targets that are peculiar to history or art, but the overall thrust must come from the leadership team. You will decide where the school is to go. You will have to ensure that it gets there.

Development planning is an ongoing process. It is never completed. Particular objectives are achieved but the plan should be under constant scrutiny, being renewed and refocused. If it is something that is done once and then looked at towards the end of its life in a climate of 'Well, how did we do?' then it was not worth it. It should be the means by which you want things to happen. You are paid to provide strategic direction so you should prepare the framework. The departments will then respond to the priorities you have set. Should you decide that 'Gifted and Talented' is a priority, the English department will indicate in their own plan how they are going to fulfil the school's objectives within their own area. Don't ask departments to set their own priorities and then try somehow to determine the school's afterwards. This is an abrogation of responsibility. You are paid handsomely to make decisions.

A development plan isn't just a list of the things that you would like to happen. It includes the big issues. You should question how it is to be achieved, what resources are needed, who is responsible for making it happen and how you will know that it has worked. This will enable you to revisit it and assess the sort of progress you are making. You will establish the school's priorities based upon your informed opinions gained through being in the school and informed by data on performance and by lesson observations. All this will indicate where improvements are needed or to be reinforced. You will need to identify how the changes are to be achieved – and this is the real challenge. Throwing more resources at an issue may not actually work. More of the same may lead to the same failure. Perhaps you need a different way of looking at things. A new approach might require visits to other schools or the purchase of new equipment. This is very likely to bring with it a training implication.

You will see how managing a school is so much easier when it is joined up – when one thing informs another. The development plan feeds inevitably into INSET. Data management feeds into the development plan. Everything feeds into and out of staffing. Always be wary of working in compartments. Even the briefest overview will show how everything links together. What any school needs is coherence and strategy. That is what you get from the development plan.

17 Using data

Data aren't an answer. They are only the beginning

Schools are awash with data. Statistics whiz backwards and forwards between schools all the time. When you receive a new student in your school, you know that there is someone somewhere who can tell you what percentage chance there is of that student achieving five C grades at GCSE. Your own school shouldn't be any different. You want to know about the profile of your Year 7? There will be data that will do just that. Want to know who is likely to achieve good grades at Key Stage 4? Look it up in the data. It is there. It is impossible to escape from. Even if you try, it will follow you home and camp on your doorstep. It might be dismal and it might feel inexorable, but you can't argue with the fact that data are very important. They give a picture of what is happening in your school and they shout at you and tell you what you should be doing.

These data will come to you in a variety of forms, as you will be aware from your previous roles in school. You need to use administrative support to maintain your database on the students and as they progress through the school you will build up a picture of their capabilities. You will of course always bear in mind that whilst some may fall short, others will exceed what is anticipated of them. This is certainly something to celebrate. It should help you to target resources and support. The data that have been gathered from previous performance over a number of years will enable comparisons to be made against the performance of very many students of similar ability from a similar background to produce statistically accurate predictions. It may not be the whole story, but it is a large part of it.

Some people love such analyses. They are very popular because they purport to give objective evidence about what is happening in the school. Data are evidence that is regarded as incontrovertible, unsullied by the vagaries of human opinion and sentiment. Let's get rid of the girlie nonsense about feelings and intuition and let's substitute some hard muscular facts. But the data you will have aren't the universal panacea and you need to interpret the data that you have in a sensitive way.

You see, all they can do is paint a picture. They don't tell you what to do. This is why you are paid as you are – to decide what needs to be done to make things better. This is where you will use your knowledge of the school and your staff. How are you going to build upon what you have and make things better? That is what it is about, prompting you to ensure that all students achieve their potential – which is fast becoming the greatest educational cliché of them all

You must ask yourself what areas of success you have in the school. What can be learnt from these successes? What help can be offered to other departments where the students are not doing quite so well? What are the inhibiting factors that exist and stand in the way of student attainment?

You will also need to understand the politics of your school. This will tell you who will learn best from whom and who is most willing to improve. There would be little purpose in throwing money and resources at the most hopeless cases. You will know who is to be encouraged and who needs to be confronted. This is where you are using your judgement and expertise. What these data will do is confirm judgements that you have already made. If data indicate a level of under-performance that you were not aware of, then you haven't been doing your job. Oh yes, the data will identify problems. But your job really is about solving them.

Data aren't an end in themselves. They are a beginning and they call for help and support from your INSET programme and your development plan. Where do the solutions lie? In training? In staffing? In expertise? In resourcing? Do you need to access external help to establish a new emphasis or direction? Or is there a source of help available within the school?

One perennial issue that the data might indicate is the disparity in the performance of boys and girls. We can take this as an example and see how we could respond to an issue indicated by the data that we hold. We can as professionals accept that this difference in achievement has always happened but we cannot accept that it must persist or that we can do nothing about it – even though there is a strong case which indicates that boys and girls learn in different ways. We all know that boys are different. You can't work in a secondary school and not realize that there are very fundamental differences between the genders. But you can't ignore it. You must recognize that the difference is there and then try to do something about it. Of course there is no magic and instant solution for everything. Everything is gradual. You need to make sure that the males in your school are role models of professionalism and achievement. The males must promote learning attitudes. You can encourage key figures amongst the student body, the influential ones, the leaders, the decision-makers. Get them on your side and focus them on learning and attainment. The others will follow.

Mentoring that involves planning and time-management advice would be especially appropriate. Regular meetings to mediate between staff and students can reduce conflict and disputes, enabling a focus on work and achievement to be maintained. This isn't necessarily the exclusive province of a deputy head but you have to be involved early on. You must provide the leadership, establishing systems, priorities and responses and making sure that they work.

This is what your job must be. Others who are paid less than you can collect and interpret data. You have to develop strategies in response to them that will support your students.

18 Managing the timetable and curriculum

The heart of the school

This has always been an aspect of the deputy head's role that has carried with it huge amounts of mystery. Deputies would often lock themselves away for weeks at a time with only a few carefully selected acolytes for company and amusement. They would move paper around, sometimes blocks of wood, sometimes pegs in a board, sometimes magnetic squares, and at the end of their allotted time emerge blinking into the sunlight, carrying with them their wisdom, etched seemingly upon steel. Great indeed was the celebration and the acclaim for a document that was full of compromises and completely inflexible, as unyielding as blocks of stone. However unsatisfactory, you had to live with it for a year until the deputy shut himself away once again.

Now we have the computer and everything is so much different. Now the emphasis has shifted from construction to design and we are all the better for it. As a deputy your job is to design a timetable that fulfils the needs of the school. And when you have done that, a computer sorts it out. Naturally a computer is only as good as the data that have been fed into it. But what the computer does is allow you to produce many different versions of your intentions. You can have more than one timetable a year if you want, in order to respond to different needs or circumstances. That mammoth task that would take weeks and was always full of irritations, is now performed instantly. You are released to concentrate upon the curriculum.

You must also ensure that you have the highest quality support that you can find to help you. It is not your job to spend your time entering data. Get someone else to help you. This frees you up to do the things you are supposed to do. As timetable software develops, then the more automated the process becomes. Less human interaction is required at the actual scheduling stage – when lessons are put on the timetable grid – to the extent that a complete timetable can be produced automatically. This puts the focus entirely upon what you should be doing, which is creating the essential building blocks of the timetable. You bring together the students and the teachers, the room and the subject, and the computer then manipulates all the different blocks to make a timetable.

The speed of the computer means that you can leave the task until even later in the school year. This means you can wait until you are clear about your staffing. You can wait until all the resignations are in and until most replacements appointed. If something dramatic happens you can re-print or even re-timetable quickly at any point in the year. This aspect of school management has been made so much easier by new technology.

The first stage in the process is the most important. That is, to establish your curriculum. What do you want to be taught and how long do you want it to be taught for? This is fundamental. This will determine the number of staff that you need and in turn will shape careers, it will influence lives.

Of course you will be unlikely to inherit a completely blank canvas. Even if your school is brand-new, you will have statutory orders with regard to curriculum time that you must fulfil. You will always be under pressure to find more time for some subjects and in fact there will usually be a strong case to be made. But if everyone can argue the case in a compelling way and if there is a finite period of time available, then you must make decisions. There will always be a head of department somewhere who wants to build an empire, because more curriculum time means more staff and a bigger budget and a shift up the staffroom pecking order. But to give one person more means that someone else has less. Not only that, your decisions will influence directly the classroom experience of your students. So always consider the consequences of any changes you make very carefully indeed. The curriculum and the timetable represent the school's purpose, so you must involve others. You will need to meet with your senior colleagues and discuss what you want, what the school needs and what the school can afford.

Early in the academic year you must assess how you are meeting the needs of your development plan and what changes you need to make to next year's curriculum in the light of this and in response to other possible pressures. These could be anticipated redundancies or retirements which, potentially, will have as big an impact as anything that else you might decide. The best way I have found is by drawing up a chart. You will find in Figure 1 an example of an old curriculum design I did for my school. The details might not be particularly relevant to you but that isn't important. Across the top you have the number of lessons that make up the timetable cycle. In this case there are 30 lessons a week. Vertically, I have placed the six registration groups in each year group, distinguished by letters A to F. Then I have arranged the curriculum for each class within this grid. Any differences in provision relate to the different nature of the classes. Students with learning difficulties are placed in classes 7E and 7F and receive less time in some subjects and more time in others. So, for example, if you look at these classes (7E and 7F) you will see that they have less Welsh for example. Why? It may have been that I wanted to put more emphasis upon the acquisition of basic skills. That would be partly true. But when I did this it was also true that I didn't have enough specialist staff to deliver Welsh. This is a perfect illustration of how staffing and curriculum are inextricably linked.

This simple chart is a powerful tool. It is not a timetable; that comes later. When you have built up your diagram for each year group in your school, you will see how many lessons you need in each subject. This chart shows you everything you need to know about how your curriculum is designed. You cannot progress until you have got this right. It will inform all the other decisions you will make.

Your next step is to total up all the lessons you need for each curriculum area and compare that total with the number that your staff can provide. There is an example from the English department in Figure 2. On the left you can see the total number of lessons that the school needs. You will see that the school offers media studies at Key Stage 4 and that this is delivered by the department. On the right you will see the number of lessons I can provide with current staffing. The totals allocated to staff reflect decisions already taken about teaching loads. Here there is a balance. To have more lessons on the right than on the left is good. To have more lessons on the left rather than the right is bad. It means that you either have to increase teaching loads or find

Year 7

Year 7	1	2	3	4	5	6	7	8	9	10	11	12	13	14	15	16	17	18	19	20	21	22	23	24	25	26	27	28	29	30
7(A)	English				Maths				Science			French		Welsh		Art		Mu	Geog		Hist		RE	IT (1/2/3)		PE (1/2/3)		DT (1/2/3)		Fp
7(B)	English				Maths				Science			French		Welsh		Art		Mu	Geog		Hist		RE							Fp
7(C)	English				Maths				Science			French		Welsh		Art		Mu	Geog		Hist		RE	IT		PE (1/2/3)		DT (1/2/3)		Fp
7(D)	English				Maths				Science			French		Welsh		Art		Mu	Geog		Hist		RE	IT						Fp

Year 7	1	2	3	4	5	6	7	8	9	10	11	12	13	14	15	16	17	18	19	20	21	22	23	24	25	26	27	28	29	30
7(E)	English					Maths			Science					IT		Art		Mu	Geog		Hist		RE	Fr	We	PE (1/3)		DT (1)		Fp
7(F)	English					Maths			Science					IT		Art		Mu	Geog		Hist		RE	Fr	We	PE (2/3)		DT (2/3)		Fp

Figure 1 Year 7 curriculum

Lessons needed

Department: English   Head of Department: CJJ   Date: June 2005

Subdivision	Number of classes or sets	Lessons per class per week	Lessons per week	Classes
Year 7x	4	4	16	1,2,3,4
Year 8x	4	3.5	14	1,2,3,4
Year 9x	5	4	20	1,2,3,4
Year 9y				
Year 10 a	5	4	20	1,2,3,4
Year 10 b	1	4	4	5
Year 10 c (MS)	2	3	6	
Year 11 a	5	4	20	1,2,3,4
Year 11 b	1	4	4	5
Year 11 c (MS)	2	3	6	
Total number of lessons required			110	

MS = media studies

Lessons that can be provided

Staff available	Subject allocation	PSD	Other subjects	Commitment	Notes
CJJ	17	1	MS6	24	
JB	24	1		25	
EW	18	1	MS6	25	
GB	15			15	
CM	24	1		25	
Total to be provided:	98		12	=	110

Figure 2 English department balance sheet

Figure 3   Whole staff allocations

Staff	1 DH	2 DL	3 JJ	4 BM	5 PP	6 DM	7 CT	8 JPD	9 LAM	10 RF	11 GT	12 CV	13 RL	14 CA	15 JB	16 EW	17 CM	18 GBR	19 AEJ	20 DD	21 WN	22 DG	23 BG	24 AL	25 FR	26 CW	27 MIE	28 JIH	29 GC	30 LM	31 SD	32 KJ	33 JMD	34 GEB	35 RU	36 JN	37 LW	38 MT	39 HC	40 AC	41 PW	42 SG	43 MW	44 JW	45 ED	46 TJ	Totals
MATHS	23	24	24	24	20	14																																							4		133
SCIENCE							23	24	24	24																																					149
ENGLISH											16	16	22			24	18	24																													98
HISTORY														17	24			15	24	24	4																										52
GEOGRAPHY																					24	24	22	24																							46
R.E.																				2				24																					4		30
TECHNOLOGY																									23	18	23	24	24	24																	95
FRENCH																															23	20															45
WELSH																														4																	43
MEDIA STUDIES															6	6																															12
PE																																	23	24	24												75
MUSIC																																			24	24											24
ART																																					20	24	16								60
IS																																						3									3
DRAMA																																							23	23	20	24	23				90
Business Studies																																									3						3
SPECIAL NEEDS																																												10	18	14	42
Total	23	24	24	24	20	18	23	24	24	24	16	16	22	23	24	24	24	24	24	24	6	24	22	24	23	18	23	24	24	24	23	24	24	24	24	24	20	24	23	23	20	24	23	14	18	14	1000
PSD	1	1	1	1	5	7	1	1	1	1				1	1	1	1	1	1	1	1	1		1	1	7	1	1	1	1	1	1	1	1	1	1	1	1	1	1	1	1	1		1	1	33
TOTAL	24	25	25	25	20	18	24	25	25	25	16	22	24	25	25	25	15	25	24	24	6	25	22	24	24	18	24	25	24	24	24	24	24	25	25	25	24	25	16	24	24	25	24	14	19	19	1033
COVER	1				5	7	1				9	3		1			10				19		3	1	1	7	1						1				1		9			1	1	11	6		117
	2	2	2	2	2	2	2	2	2	2	2	2	2	2	2	2	2	2	2	2	2	2	2	2	2	2	2	2	2	2	2	2	2	2	2	2	2	2	2	2	2	2	2	2	2	2	92
NON-CONTACT	3	3	3	3	3	3	3	3	3	3	3	3	3	3	3	3	3	3	3	3	3	3	3	3	3	3	3	3	3	3	3	3	3	3	3	3	3	3	3	3	3	3	3	3	3	3	138
TOTAL	30	30	30	30	30	30	30	30	30	30	30	30	30	30	30	30	30	30	30	30	30	30	30	30	30	30	30	30	30	30	30	30	30	30	30	30	30	30	30	30	30	30	30	30	30	30	1380

another set of initials to add to the department. In this particular case
there were no other staff available to teach English so I increased my
own teaching commitment by four lessons per week in order to achieve
a balance. Down these mean streets a deputy must walk.

You must then transfer these teaching loads to a master chart which
is illustrated in Figure 3. It is by shuffling numbers about on a chart like
this that you will eventually discover a balance, if indeed there is one
there. It is on this chart that you can see where there is a surplus, where
there is a deficit and where you are going to ask staff to teach outside
their subject area if that is necessary.

Once you have established your curriculum in this way you can
give heads of department details of what lessons you want them to teach
and they can then assign teachers' initials against them. The scheduling
part of the process can then begin. The requirements will be determined
by the computer system you are using and are not really appropriate to
this book.

Never think that doing the timetable is a once-only process. It is not.
You need to try out different models through the year until you find
one that you are happy with. As the year goes on you will be involved
in these discussions and it is on such simple charts as these that you can
determine the consequences. English results are good. Mathematics
results are poor. Why? Do you need to increase curriculum time for
mathematics? Will this make any difference? Are you providing more
opportunities for syllabus coverage? Or are you merely providing more
of what wasn't working in the first place? If you make changes what
will the effect on staffing be? Can you staff any of the changes you
make? Where will the additional lessons come from?

You decide that you want to make German compulsory. You collect
all your arguments and present them. You will need resources to do it.
Where from? By phasing out the astrology department. Suddenly you
are dealing with people, their income, their way of life, their hopes
and expectations, their state of mind. Don't ever think that these little
charts are just pieces of paper.

In the case of the astrology department this is, surprisingly, something
that they hadn't anticipated. It will be painful and difficult. But whatever
happens, remember that the needs of the school always come first.
When the governors appointed you they decided to back your judgement. Schools are not run for the staff. They are run for the students

and to serve their needs. You are a key figure in determining what those needs are.

There are lots of things you can do with a timetable. After all, it is merely a way of getting students into lessons at different times of the day in order to fulfil learning objectives. There are many ways of doing this. You can have a six-day timetable, ten days, a floating day six. You can have periods of different lengths within the day. You can mix single lessons with doubles or triples. I have always taken the view that it is best to keep it as simple as possible. You do not want the timetable to get in the way of the curriculum. So when you take up your post, don't change things for the sake of it. Don't introduce a wildly complex timetable merely to show that you have arrived. Do what you do for a reason that you understand, and that you can justify.

It is the curriculum that is important. The simplistic analysis is that we try to fit all children into the curriculum, whereas we ought really to fit the curriculum around the children. Sadly this is largely impractical. We group students together in order to teach them and achieve economies of scale. Inevitably compromises are made. Perhaps our curriculum should be more flexible and involve more choices, but this is very expensive. Any expansion of provision that might be desirable would bring with it staffing costs. These are, naturally, very high and long-term. You can't keep chopping and changing your staff on short-term contracts to meet constantly changing needs. Teachers need continuity of employment and security and the result of this is a compromise in terms of the curriculum offered. And once you have that member of staff you will probably ensure that there are students there for them to teach. This is an inbuilt reason why schools don't change as quickly as some people would like. Obviously you will try to stay aware and flexible and offer as wide a range of opportunities as you can. But the core of what you offer needs to remain the same, unless you embark upon huge re-training programmes which would be expensive, the consequences of which would be uncertain.

Your fundamental principle has to be entitlement. All students have an entitlement to the same curriculum, whether they want it or not. To make choices about what will be studied too early in one's career could have serious consequences. It could easily establish a two-tier education provision – with some experiences, such as foreign languages and English literature, denied to some and not to others. How can anyone be sure of what shape their life will take in their early teenage years? To throw yourself too soon on to a specific vocational tramline could be a mistake. You might choose the wrong vocational route and then you would be locked into a long-term mistake. So, whilst the shift towards vocational pathways appears to be a seductive one, there are real reservations that need to be explored.

An example would be to take the study of literature out of the KS4 English curriculum in your school and make it instead an optional choice. What would this mean? The study of Shakespeare or poetry would become a marginal pursuit. Such a decision would deny the right of all to understand their heritage, and close down that opportunity for reflection that great writers give us. Of course, some students would reject such an opportunity at the earliest opportunity but it doesn't mean to say that they would be right to do so.

The right of a child to choose what they study needs to be introduced gradually, without irrevocable decisions being taken too early. There should be a gradual shift in emphasis in the curriculum which would be based upon knowledge and an evolving sense of a career path, but students should never be labelled as hairdressers or plumbers too soon. I have taught in schools which are regarded as serving challenging areas and I know how difficult it can be when awkward and disruptive students are following courses that they don't like. But you can have no reassurance that their behaviour would be any different elsewhere or in a different classroom. They are, after all, still children and still need the guidance of their teachers. To make them follow vocational courses that would in the end restrict their intellectual choices would be a real mistake.

19 Dealing with finances and the budget

It is not your job to make a profit

What is this about in the context of a school? The budget exists as a tool for ensuring that a proper education is delivered to all students. That's all. You are not a business. You are responsible for expenditure but have less control over income. You can't generate substantial amounts of money unless student numbers rise significantly or unless you hit upon some sort of astonishing idea that other schools want to buy, such as a study programme, or if you can earn rental income for the use of your buildings, or from a Christmas park and ride scheme. But what else can you do? After all, selling Year 10 into slavery is generally regarded as unacceptable by the majority of parents. You are a teacher, not an accountant and your responsibility is to deploy the money the school receives to educate its students. Of course, arrangements vary from school to school and in different areas of the country. Funding regimes vary enormously because there is such variety in the nature of schools. Some schools will run their own budgets and delegate that responsibility to a member of the leadership team. Others will indeed employ bursars and accountants. But the principle remains unchanged. You don't have to make a profit. You are not a business. You may adopt models of business efficiency but your primary purpose is a school. The students who come to you only get one chance and you need to deploy resources to ensure that chance is a good one. The benefits that come from educating someone properly are long-term. There is no instant return, for education is truly an investment.

You need to use the money in order to serve the needs of the school as defined in your development plan. It is also important to guarantee a range of experiences to your students so that they can have a full and rounded education. But your job is more than just dividing the money up. It is more than slicing up a cake. By reinforcing the development plan you can influence the direction the school is taking.

When you examine the details of the school budget it is clear that the majority of the school's money is spent on salaries. It is people that make schools work. So you have a responsibility to ensure that the people you have are used effectively and that they make a worthwhile contribution. And, if you need to save large amounts of money because of a financial difficulty, then you will need to look at the staffing budget. You will not save much by reducing departmental capitation or by cutting expenditure on pest control. There is a belief that you can reduce any budget by 1 per cent and not seriously affect quality. Many small reductions can add up to a big saving. But remember, you are not a profit-making organization. You do not serve a balance sheet. You serve people and that is never a cheap option.

The most important thing in the classroom is the teacher. It is your job to get the best teachers you can, maintain them, support them and get them in the right classroom with the right students. Then productive learning will take place.

Ultimately then other resources are less important than your staff. It does make sense. Put all the books and equipment you like in a classroom and nothing will happen. They will never make a poor teacher better. The mere provision of resources will never guarantee quality. What matters is how the resources are used and how they are matched to student needs. And also whether or not the teacher is prepared to use them efficiently. How the resources are used could suggest that specific training needs must be addressed. If the use of a computer is vital, then the teacher must be able to use it or must show a genuine willingness to learn. You must use the budget to invest in all the people who use your school in whatever capacity, either as teachers or as learners.

You are not an accountant. Neither are most of the others who will examine what the school does. So you need to prepare something by which others can see quickly and unambiguously where the money in the school goes. You have to be transparent, not least because your responsibility must always be for teaching and learning. So keep your financial arrangements simple. This can be particularly helpful for the governing body, many of whom will have little experience of dealing with large amounts of money.

The school receives its money from whatever source and what the leadership team must do is divide it up between the different categories that together make up the totality of the institution. What you can do is show everyone how much you need to run the school. Then you can balance this against the money you receive. You can see an example of this in Figure 4. This is a copy of the sort of budget sheet I have used. I have changed the figures and removed elements of income that are part of our individual relationship with the LEA, so the figure here isn't entirely accurate. It is the shape that is important. The income is what you see on the left. On the right you will see how I divided up the money that we received. My budget statement for the governors had ten pages, each one outlining a different area of expenditure.

To explain further the areas of expenditure, which you should detail on individual sheets (see Figure 4):

1. is the most important one. Staffing costs
2. is the money required to run subject areas and departments. It is such a small part of the overall sum received
3. includes money to pay examination entry fees
4. is money set aside to pay for elements such as Home Tuition or for students attending behavioural units
5. pays for telephones and postage
6. covers a whole host of items such as money paid back to the LEA for the services they provide
7. is a projection of what will be needed to pay for gas and electricity
8. covers general repairs, adaptations and improvements, health and safety issues. As buildings gets older so such costs increase
9. is what we paid for cleaning, waste disposal and grounds maintenance
10. covers security costs and the rates bill

Schools are very different and such divisions may not suit your circumstances. But these worked for us and the principle of splitting up your expenditure into parts that can be easily understood is something you can employ.

LEA Income

Allocation received from the LEA	£2,745,718	
Additional funding from LEA	£39,321	
Total		**£2,785,039**

Other income sources (estimates)

Bank interest	£8,000	
Rent	£8,000	
Miscellaneous	£30,000	
Total		**£46,000**

Total income	**£2,831,039**

Area of expenditure		Expenditure	Balance
Teaching costs	*Sheet 1*		£371,100
Administration staff	*Sheet 1*		£314,250
Other support staff	*Sheet 1*	£2,459,939	£258,461
Capitation	*Sheet 2*	£56,850	£248,461
Academic services	*Sheet 3*	£55,789	£237,961
Student services	*Sheet 4*	£10,000	£84,182
Communications	*Sheet 5*	£10,500	£40,182
Support services	*Sheet 6*	£153,779	-£20,818
Energy	*Sheet 7*	£44,000	-£120,818
Maintenance	*Sheet 8*	£61,000	-£187,953
Contracts	*Sheet 9*	£100,000	
Other premises costs	*Sheet 10*	£67,135	
Total expenditure		**£3,018,992**	
Carry forward Figure		**-£187,953**	

Figure 4   School budget

In the example here you will see a large shortfall. The real budget on which this example is based did, in fact, produce a shortfall. Not as extreme as the one here but significant enough nonetheless. If there is a shortfall you have a problem that you need to resolve. Good housekeeping will save you a little but there is only one way to sort out a bigger deficit and that is by reducing your staffing bill. This may be through redundancy or retirement. Of course, this is what we had to do. But whatever happens, your job is to minimize the effect this might have upon the curriculum. That is your duty.

As far as departmental capitation is concerned you will act as chancellor and everyone else in the school will try to get more money out of you. Your job is to maintain an overview and you mustn't allow yourself to be conned. Yes, the head of mathematics has had a good idea, perhaps for the first time, but then so have others. So you need to employ a formula for an equitable and transparent allocation, though you must leave yourself with room for manoeuvre. An expensive piece of capital expenditure might be needed in one department as a matter of urgency that could overturn your structures. You could, for example, ask them to repay a loan from their capitation over a period of three years. Obviously, some areas like technology are particularly expensive to run. Be prepared to invest in the things that you think are important.

Be careful of bidding procedures. You could certainly find a good idea attached to a poorly written bid and a poor idea supported by a high-quality presentation. So make sure you assess the idea, not the quality of the bid from someone who isn't very good at putting them together. When I was a head of department I was hopeless at it. You were appointed because of your vision, so don't be afraid to show it. You need to be clear about what you want and the direction you believe the school should be going. That might require either additional funds or imaginative accounting. If you allocate money to something then immediately it becomes important, in the same way as making a teacher responsible for something. Put extra money into mythology and suddenly the department has great importance. Fund another teacher and suddenly careers are being built, promotion sought. Money makes things happen and is the articulation of your ideas.

Like the majority of schools we use a formula to distribute money. We give a threshold figure to every department to underpin what they do. Then there needs to be an additional sum determined by the number of staff in the department and the number of rooms a department must maintain. A calculation is then required, based upon the number of students taking the subject. All this information comes from the curriculum. You can then make a further adjustment for departments such as art and technology that incur additional expenses because their department requires a heavy expenditure on consumable items. It is always a good idea to publish a list that shows how the cake has been cut up. Departments may not be happy with the money they have received but at least they will be able to understand the process.

Of course, you can, as a leadership team, move on to another level. If you want to explore issues like value for money, then you can calculate how much it costs to deliver each subject. Include staffing costs, supply cover and suddenly you get a very different picture. This is what it really costs to deliver a subject. What does the school receive in return for such expenditure? Sometimes a nasty shock. Link this with data of pupil performance and you might have to reassess your priorities. Of course you might not be able to do so entirely. But this might help you to target training.

One particularly tricky issue is pay. You will be in a position where you might be contributing to the determination of your own pay. It is not a very comfortable position. Your pay must be reviewed annually and the ethical pressure, either unspoken or otherwise, is not to take an increase on the occasions when the school is in difficulty. Yet why should you sacrifice your position and that of your family, when other staff are not expected to do so? Maintaining differentials is ultimately the key. Your pay should move in line with that of other staff, so that differentials are not eroded. This happens in the determination of your own pay in relation to the headteacher's salary. The same thing should happen between leadership pay and that of the other staff.

When you start dealing with staff salaries you are suddenly dealing with staff destinies, their sense of self-worth and their status. Decisions that appear logical and incontrovertible to you can suddenly explode in your face where money is concerned. What you will soon discover is that the perceptions of staff about themselves and the job they do don't necessarily match yours. Teachers might feel they are underpaid, that what they do isn't recognized. And they might be right. But you have to operate within financial constraints. You can't award pay rises merely for long service or to boost a pension. Whatever you do must be related to your development plan. This is why it is so important, because it shows where the school wants to go and is a justification of the decisions you make. If you have said in the plan that you want mythology to become compulsory in Year 10, then no one can complain when you appoint more mythology teachers and promote the head of department. Of course they will complain. Almost everyone wants to be paid more. If all jobs lie somewhere along a continuum that stretches from the hell of doing everything and being paid nothing to the nirvana of doing nothing and being paid everything, then many spend their lives trying to move further up the stairway to heaven. After all, promotion is still perceived by some as an opportunity to be paid more for doing less. As a manager in the school you will be acutely aware of the absurdity of this stance and also how you must ensure value for money. Of course, you don't want to get things done on the cheap. You want to pay your staff the proper rate for the job that they do. But you also need to be reassured that the salaries you are paying are actually having a positive influence in the classroom. Because if they don't then you are throwing your precious money away. Things are changing. Short-term enhancements and contracts tied to performance are all part of a flexible approach. You will always want to recognize quality, commitment and performance amongst your staff. You don't want to feel that you can't reward young talent simply because all the school's money is tied up in immovable upgradings awarded years ago. Vibrant teaching is thus undervalued; unimaginative time-servers thus overpaid. So you will need to keep yourself informed about what is possible. Look at contractual details and opportunities presented in the *School Teachers' Pay and Conditions Document.*

As time goes on we are moving away from permanent salary enhancements. Now we can see increases tied to specific projects and initiatives. Whether this is better or not is not a debate for this book but you can do it. It shows that your development plan lies at the heart of your leadership decisions. It excuses you from having to justify why you won't award a pay rise to the head of pottery. The governors made mythology a priority. Of course, when you say no it may be the opportunity you were looking for to discuss their shortcomings. Or it may not be the right moment. In which case say that their pay does not yet fit in with the school's priorities. But when we are talking about money in this way it is rare indeed for the disappointed to rise smiling and shake your hand, suddenly transformed by the purity of your vision. Rather, they are straight on the phone to their professional association.

The answer in the end lies in that teacher's own hands. If they are not happy they can look for a job elsewhere and test the market. There is nothing wrong with teachers looking for promotion. If they have done a good job then they will leave with your support and thanks. It is a normal part of the profession and it is how schools develop and how departments refresh themselves. But never let a teacher hold a gun to your head. A teacher might tell you that they won't apply for that job in a neighbouring school if you give them a pay rise. You can't respond. Wish them luck and offer them whatever support you can. But don't offer them money. Call their bluff. See if they are serious. Because if you don't then you will have everyone knocking on your door, testing you out. Since salaries are the key to the budget, there is constant pressure to force them down. It is a way of getting more teachers for the same overall money or less. So when a teacher leaves don't automatically replace them with someone on an identical salary. Perhaps over the years the job has changed and it no longer justifies the level of pay. Perhaps the subject is no longer as important as it once was. So assess the job and assess the marketplace. Make sure you are paying the correct rate for the job. But also remember if you undervalue the job your field of applicants will inevitably be restricted. At the same time, whilst you will want to recognize your staff and what they do, if you pay them too much they will never move and you will have to deal with a rump of staff too ready to inhabit the deckchairs, watching the icebergs float by.

20 Evaluating your school

If you don't know your own school, then who does?

Apparently, a report to the United States Congress in 1992 said 'We must learn to measure what we value rather than valuing what we can easily measure.' It may have been written some time ago now but it still holds true. Often in our eagerness to make a complex job simple, we get things back to front.

When you make judgements about your school you must do so based on the things that matter, primarily the learning that takes place in the classroom. This must remain your main motivation – the need to discharge your responsibility to the students and their community. In order to do this you have to gather information about how well teachers and their students are performing and then evaluate it. Your purpose in doing this? It is quite simple: to help the teachers who want to do their job better. You can help by offering advice, opportunities for training and resources.

The best teachers do this all the time. They have a commitment that leads them to reflect in a critical way on their practice. This is what being a professional means. You must ask yourself 'What do I need to do to improve my performance?' Some teachers will need help with this but self-evaluation is a critical aspect of life in school. Lessons must be observed, documentation analysed and assessed, marking and assessment examined. There must be a school policy on the issue so that all staff are treated equitably, without any feeling of paranoia. Many of your staff will welcome such scrutiny, but whatever their personal feelings, it has to happen. You must not rely upon an external inspection process to carry this out. You must be involved in a system that is part of the fabric of school life. Making judgements should not be a huge and occasional festival of anxiety.

You must always ensure that you have sufficient time and energy to put any plans into effect. There is no point in creating some vast bureaucracy that will capsize under its own weight. Whatever you do must be manageable. As far as lesson observations are concerned, you could design your own forms to be used by observers. It might, however, make more sense to use those that will be used in external inspections. Their value is that they provide the absolute focus that you need. They will ensure that you concentrate upon the fundamental issue of learning. They can restore any unnoticed drifting in your priorities. There is an art in completing lesson observation forms that comes with practice – making sure that your thoughts are recorded in the right place will enable you to draw effective conclusions by structuring your impressions for you. In this way the form will illuminate your instinctive observations. It is another example of the fact that whatever you do in school must be structured.

What should be clear is that the context of any evaluation process that you carry out in your school must be firmly established. You need to know what you are evaluating, why you are doing it and with whom you will share the information. Of course, the audience must primarily be an internal one. You might decide to share the findings, if needed, with outside interests like inspectors and the LEA, but really it is about the school looking at what it is doing so that it can do it better. The results of your evaluations will determine the way the school is managed, initiatives undertaken, the way finances are distributed and the areas to which new staff are appointed. They will be extremely important.

Always have faith in your teachers. They do not need to be watched all the time. It is not the thought of lesson observation that keeps chaos at bay. The lessons and the school continue at their own pace quite naturally. The timetable and the programmes of study should move things along in their own inevitable way. You need to have a structure in place that is part of the dialogue that links leadership with the middle managers. They need to be involved in managing their part of the school and they need to know how they fit into the overall vision of the institution. A line management system is an ideal way of achieving this. Middle managers are the ones with the expert knowledge of their area. It is what they are paid for. They should report progress to the leadership team. You can't be expected to retain all the specific details of a department's scheme of work. What you do need to know are the particular pressure points that might exist – the things the department finds difficult or which pose particular problems – especially as these might impact upon resources. Your middle managers are paid to exercise that subject expertise and you need to create a forum in which they can connect positively with the leadership of the school.

What will inform your judgements is your overall knowledge of the school. You will be able to celebrate its strengths and also to address its weaknesses. Your position makes you uniquely informed and makes your judgements much more valuable than any formulated by any external inspector. It is for this reason that an internal review is far more effective and influential than any external one. Any external evaluation can only ever be a dipstick, indicating the levels on a particular day, with a report written with judgements based on this experience. You, on the other hand, will have a much more coherent picture of school performance because you will have a greater awareness since you will be doing it all the time. So if you are doing your job properly then all an inspection will do is to confirm your judgements. It can verify and authenticate and give you the confidence to move on. But an inspection is no substitute for the real thing. Your opinions are much more valuable because they have been formed over a longer period and upon the basis of detailed understanding.

This really is the role of external inspections: they are part of a process. They are not the whole of a process. They provide external criteria to validate internal priorities. Our schools must be able to offer their own articulated evaluation of how well they are performing and have the courage to act upon their findings.

Schools should not deny the importance of an inspection process. People have a right to know what is going on in our schools and that our students are enjoying a worthwhile experience. But they should never throw up anything that the leadership team doesn't already know. If it does then the leadership team is failing in a sadly spectacular way.

21 Improving an underachieving department

A fundamental responsibility

The most important thing you must do is to accept that things need changing when indeed they do. This is the crucial first step. Until it is made, the long march towards improvement and success can never begin. There are many ways that you might do this, though the trigger is often some sort of crisis like a failed inspection. If you have been doing your job properly then you will have anticipated the problem some time before. Failure is not something that people will always recognize in themselves. They will look for external explanations and blame others – the students, leadership, the system. You will have made a judgement based upon your observations and awareness but the legitimacy of your opinions might only be accepted following a damning report. Too often the poor opinion of the leadership team is dismissed as being ill-informed or malicious. Your quality assurance programme should have informed your view and you should then have raised concerns. They might go through the motions of changing things but may only embrace the urgency when someone new tells them that frankly they stink. There are different reasons why a department may be in difficulties. Never be so quick as to dismiss the part that the leadership team could have played. Are staffing and resources adequate? Have you failed to deal with a difficult staffing issue? Is a weak teacher, who you appointed, dragging the department down? Be ready to analyse what you have done. Has it been effective and supportive? If it hasn't been, then what sort of purpose does the leadership team serve?

You might need to examine timetabling arrangements. Are these contributing to the problems? If so, what can you do? Don't forget, the timetable may seem fixed in September but it can be changed if there is an issue. Obviously it is not straightforward and it will affect a lot of others because of the way it is interlinked, but if the timetable is wrong then do something about it. Don't throw your hands up in the air and say it is impossible. Your job as deputy head is to find solutions. Effective change must be based upon honesty. It is part of a process of openness. You are acknowledging that things aren't right and that things need to change. To this end you are playing your part by changing the timetable. The head of department should play their part too.

Examine all issues carefully. The reasons for underachievement are often complex but a weak head of department is often the key. A good head of department will already have found ways of dealing with an underperformer and is likely to have involved you in the process. No, the most common cause of problems is weak leadership. This is often a very difficult issue to deal with, especially if the person is older and ostensibly more experienced than you are. They may feel unhappy about taking advice and criticism from someone they regard as a jumped-up careerist. But remember that your appointment has conferred such seniority upon you.

This can be very frustrating for other, more junior, members of the area. If you have others who are anxious for change they will welcome your intervention. It will help their professional development and make them feel better about themselves. They have been unable to implement change and it requires your intervention to give the focus and to make it happen. It might feel awkward but you can achieve lasting improvement by leading staff, by taking responsibility, not by shirking it. You need to focus upon the needs of the students, not upon the feelings of the teachers.

At the same time, in order to be effective you must filter the information you receive and recognize bias. You need to use the information you have and decide what is objective evidence. Gather the evidence properly. You will have formed an instinctive impression from your tours around the school. That gut instinct is almost certainly correct. But it needs to be backed up. Don't rely on gossip from other members of staff or from learning support assistants. They do know what is going on but you need to address your role professionally.

You must meet with the departmental leader to air your concerns. Plan your meeting carefully and in a structured way. Plan what you are going to say and don't end the meeting until you have said what you want to say. Give yourself plenty of time, get cover for lessons if you have to, because you do not wish to be rushed. Make sure that you meet in a comfortable space – but it has to be your space. You set the agenda, you establish the tone. Always show a willingness to listen but never allow any argument to be pursued that suggests the students are entirely to blame. That will never do. Try to avoid words like 'failing' and 'weak'. Inspector-speak never goes down well. Instead use words like 'issues', 'improvement', 'progress' and 'sharing'. You are trying to establish a shared view of their role and of the issues that trouble you.

Prior to this meeting it can be useful to ask the head of department to write down their ideas about the issue. What do you think are the components of the perfect science lesson, for example? Then compare their ideas with yours. The common ground gives you somewhere to start and you can match that up against the reality of performance. The bits that are left out can be equally revealing. You can then establish whether the head of department is ready to make the steps necessary to change in order to fulfil your now-agreed expectations. Don't be afraid of doing this. Your seniority confers upon you the right to say that you are unhappy about something; indeed you have a duty to say so.

Your strategy has been to gather the information and make a judgement about what needs to be done. Now you must find examples of good practice that can be shared, both inside and outside the school. Plan visits and INSET, establishing resource and staffing issues. You are working together but you might have to set the pace. If the head of department were able to sort this out for themselves then they would have done it sooner.

In some way or other you will have to invest in the area that is causing you concern. This is why you carry out your monitoring functions – to indicate how resources should be targeted. The days of the blind and annual equitable distribution of money to all departments may need to be reviewed. Resources might need to be invested in an area to bring it up to standard in order to fulfil your obligations to the student body. Invest where the need is greatest, if you can.

A significant indicator in a failing department is unpopularity amongst the students themselves. They know what's going on. They know what is best for them and, whilst a few may relish chaos and under-achievement in the short term, it won't last. Like devils sick of sin most will realize they prefer to be taught in lessons that are successful and enjoyable.

You need to be able to extract the information from your management procedures, your meetings, your observations and your audits. This should identify good practice within a department that can be shared or good practice in another department that can be transferred. You should have a programme of lesson observations and peer observations in place. Staff should be familiar with the idea of being watched. Allow them to watch each other, to share good practice. Give the observations a focus if you need to, perhaps looking at the end of lessons or at group work. Find centres of good practice that staff can visit but make sure that when they go they know precisely what they are looking for. You might need to shift their attention away from resourcing, because this is generally a means of shifting responsibility away from the real problem. It is too easy to say that more successful teachers are better resourced. If it was only ever resourcing then that is very simple to resolve and you would need to ask yourself why it hasn't happened sooner. There will be a need to look at more fundamental things. Change is needed in the mind and in the heart.

When staff return from a visit you need to meet them. Ask for a report – just a brief outline will do. After all, the school has made an investment. Then together explore the issues that have arisen. Agree an action plan, determine responsibilities. They may need time for further INSET and you should try to provide it. You have already recognized that this is a priority by sending them on this visit. So you need to be ready to respond. Don't expect everything to turn around immediately. Proper embedded improvement takes time. Focus upon staged improvement. Decide who will take responsibility for each action and determine what they need. Your role is to provide the support to make it happen and the most important thing you will achieve is an acceptance that things must change. You don't want a cosmetic agreement that there is a problem if it is merely a way of making the issue go away. The desire to change must be the teachers'. Without it then little progress will be made. But if they cannot fulfil your expectations then it may be necessary for them to look for a post elsewhere.

22 Making appointments

Structure your instincts

The days of the cosy chat in the overheated headmaster's office are gone. Things are much more professional now. Of course it doesn't always make the process of appointing staff any more reliable. However sophisticated the process, it is still not an exact science. It never can be. Mistakes are made in every school and we all have to live with the consequences of them. What you need is a system that tries to minimize them. You want to attract the best and deter those who are not suitable. What you are trying to do is to look into the future and determine job success and assess compatibility between the person and the different elements in the organization. It isn't easy.

Your purpose when making an appointment is to ensure smooth transitions. The efficient replacement of one with another ensures that there is managed change and a sense of improvement. You need to get your procedures right so that you are appointing the sort of people that will make the good things happen.

You will spend a great deal of time seeking out the best appointments. It is not merely about appointing a new head of mathematics. You also need to establish a procedure for finding, keeping and managing supply teachers, for example. Such appointments often happen in desperate circumstances and you don't want to offer someone a position hastily and live to regret it bitterly. You may need to consider offering the post for a month or half a term. This way both parties have the chance to get out of the arrangement with honour if it doesn't work out. You might not relish having to start out all over again, but sometimes it just has to be done. A poor appointment of a temporary member of staff can wreak untold damage to a school.

Don't forget either that you will not only be appointing teachers. Lots of others work in your school. Your processes need to be professional at all times but the demands will be different. Generally, the simpler the job, the simpler the procedures.

To do any of this properly you will need to be interested in people, have a desire to find out about them and the ability to allow candidates to reveal their qualities through well-planned questions. Don't forget that your governors may have a range of valuable and appropriate experiences that they can bring to the process. Don't look upon them as an irrelevance. Like you, they will want the best appointment for the school, and whilst the leadership team may have the professional experience, governors can still contribute by asking an unexpected or searching question or by spotting something you have overlooked. Why shouldn't they be involved anyway? They will be legally responsible for any appointment made. They represent the community whose needs the teacher will want to serve. They have an investment in getting it right. Naturally they will need to declare any personal interest to make sure no one else benefits personally from the appointment, otherwise it cannot be presented as being made impartially. Generally speaking, they will defer to the head's professional judgement but they can provide an independent voice and balance.

The first thing you have to do quite clearly is establish what it is that you want when someone leaves. Do you want a straight replacement or is this an opportunity to effect much-needed curriculum change? Next you need to get your advert right. Is it clearly defining what the job is and who should apply? Look at advertisements for similar posts. Examine national standards, where available. Make sure that you don't establish discriminatory procedures. It would be regarded as odd to advertise for a mathematics teacher solely in a publication aimed at the gay community. It would be equally foolish to exclude any candidates in other parts of the process.

The documentation you send out is very important. It allows candidates to make an informed judgement and helps in marketing the school. They become public documents and so you want them to reflect the very best things about your school. The job description and the person specification are crucial in offering the proper encouragement to the genuine candidates you seek.

This is all part of the procedure and should be clear and supportive, whoever you are trying to appoint. If you get these elements working successfully and you find that you have a good field, then you will have a range of good candidates who will be right for the job but in their different ways. You will be able to see how an agenda for change could be set. If you don't get that range, then it will be difficult and you could be forced by circumstances into a particular decision.

When you look at application forms bear in mind that laws change. The circumstances that once led to criminal conviction may no longer be unlawful. Changing attitudes towards homosexuality are a good example. So don't immediately reject a candidate because they carry with them irrelevant historical residue. Always be seen to appoint on merit. Don't always reject the candidate who stole a loaf of bread in hungry student days.

When candidates arrive they need to be given a comfortable base for the day, where they can rest between engagements. Refreshments and newspapers need to be available. Make sure that your catering arrangements don't discriminate against anyone with particular dietary requirements that might be associated with their religion or belief. Just remember how stressful an occasion it can be and remember that you need to create a supportive environment in which candidates can show the qualities you seek, such as integrity, respect, a sense of duty. It will be hard to show such qualities if you don't know where to find the toilet. They should be given a tour of all parts of the school. After all, you have nothing to hide. Don't forget, however, that it can be a tricky issue. Local candidates might phone up and ask for a tour of the school before the interview day. I have never been entirely comfortable with this. For them, this visit can become a part of the interview, a time when they get your undivided attention. This might act to the disadvantage of distant candidates who, through necessity, can only turn up on the day itself.

Different interview panels exploring different aspects of the job are a good idea. Your aim is to select someone who can meet all your criteria. So you will establish indicators, triggers that will inform your decision. These might be words or concepts that are mentioned. Generally these can be spotted easily and registered. You might end up with a column of ticks but this does not always mean the candidate is the right person for the position. You will have to use your judgement to decide whether they will fit in or not. They will become part of your team and you need to feel that they will both fit in and bring something to it.

Questions or tasks should be designed to check for skills and competences. You mustn't be tempted to ask personal questions that could be intrusive and suggest potential discrimination. Childcare arrangements should not be your concern, for example. Interviewers can pool their findings at the end of a session and will find that a full picture of a candidate emerges from the different perspectives. What you do have to bear in mind is that the more staff you involve – and it can be a valuable staff-development activity – the more disruption to the daily life of the school there is. You have to balance this out, since there will be even more disruption to the school if you appoint the wrong person.

Remember, however, that interviews are often poor predictors of future performance, since there is little relationship between the events in the interview room and future events in the classroom. All you can do in the end is make an informed guess. Yes, it is an act of faith. A leap into the unknown.

A teaching exercise is now almost a standard part of appointment procedures. It is something that you need to use with caution. I know good teachers who appear to have underperformed on the teaching exercise because it can be the arena of the Flash Harry or Harriet. Remember, the teacher is performing outside normal parameters. No relationships have been established, no assessments made, no continuity created. So treat it with caution, or all our schools will be staffed by performance teachers, smart and loud but insubstantial. Certainly, job sampling has its place. This is where candidates carry out part of the job, rather than just talk about it. A typist, for example, needs to show they can word-process. If you want a music teacher who plays the piano this is the way you might establish that you are not appointing a guitarist.

Appointments are time-consuming and soak up a lot of resources. They are expensive: advertising costs, travel and accommodation, covering lessons for significant staff. But it is vital that you get the right person. They will help to drive the school forward. The wrong appointment will anchor you to the rocks. It can be very frustrating when, after investing considerable time and resources in a new appointment, the realization slowly dawns that you might have got it wrong. Sometimes no amount of retraining or realignment can sort this out. Staffing costs are a school's greatest expense. You need to invest to get it right. And you also need to trust to your instincts.

23 Training your staff

Value your most expensive asset

You will find references to this throughout this book because it will be one of your primary responsibilities. You must be fully involved in training and guiding your staff. There should be no topic upon which you are not prepared to become an expert. A good example of this would be pensions. As the staff in your school get older they will want some up-to-date advice about the system and their entitlements. They might well turn to you. If you are going to manage your staff properly you will acquire this knowledge. There should be no topic about which you cannot offer expert advice. It is part of being a leader. It is important to your staff. Your involvement in their training needs lends credibility both to you and to the subject, because you will be seen to be encouraging a practical school focus.

Always be ready to give feedback, both to your teaching colleagues as well as the leadership team, when you come back from a course. It is a sign of confidence in your staff that you want to share these things with them, and many of them will regard these occasions as an opportunity to watch you doing your work. Your delivery, however, must be good. If it is, it will become the bedrock of your reputation. It is a skill that you must develop. Research your topic, obviously, and practise what you want to say. It could be a presentation on your timetable or on the budget or on lesson observations, but never do it casually. Your reputation is on the line every time you speak to the staff, whether in a meeting or at the morning bulletin, so always take it seriously. Get things wrong – no matter what the situation – and there will be those who will always remember.

Obviously you will need to use the technology available that will make your presentation interesting, but always be ready for it to break down. Don't let yourself be stranded by a dodgy plug. Technology can add a highly professional gloss to a presentation. But a slick performance should never be more important than what you say. Obviously, it is like technological toys in the classroom: they augment the teacher, they can never replace them. Once the medium starts to be more important than the message then we have a problem.

There is often a problem with training since it is not always spread equally amongst staff. If your development plan is working properly then this is not going to be the case. There might be a particular need that should be addressed at a particular time, and so other things will not have the same priority. You can't split a limited training budget uniformly or equally, and one year cannot always mirror what went before. This will upset some staff who might feel that their own pro-fessional development is thus being marginalized. But you can always refer them to the plan which maps out your priorities as a school. This avoids a suggestion that you have favourites who get on courses and others who do not.

Naturally you have to monitor staff training to make sure that you don't have teachers who are like waiters. You need to catch their eye quickly between courses or they will have gone. There may be others who need training opportunities but are perhaps less assertive. Again, this is where your plan is important. It establishes focused priorities, not random ones. And whilst you will want to encourage your staff to progress in their careers and you will understand the benefits that INSET will bring, school priorities are more important than individual ones. Personal goals and ambitions are often best served in courses that run outside the school day. During the day the classroom must always be a priority and so any course that takes a teacher away from that must be a worthwhile one.

Your responsibility too is not just to your school. It is to the profession as a whole. You need to ensure that there will be staff who can become deputies after you. Never assume that no one else could possibly do your job. Never assume that level of superiority. Give staff an opportunity to see what you are doing through projects and through shadowing. Always keep your staff informed about the decisions you are making. Setting up a working party can be a way of doing this, but such a group must have some power with which to influence events. Teachers hate the idea of a talking shop. Too many committees are bad, because in the end you cannot deny that one of your primary functions is making decisions. Informed ones yes, but ultimately your stamp needs to be on decisions that are taken. You cannot always be referring what you must do to other people.

A particularly effective means of training is actually to involve your staff in the mentoring of trainee teachers and of newly qualified teachers. Whenever a teacher speaks to a trainee they are thinking about what they are doing and why it is that they do it. To be involved with the new generation is always refreshing and it can reinvigorate those who haven't given much time to reflection. It helps to anchor the future of our job to the priorities and techniques of today. It should be regarded as a privilege and a duty to be involved. All you need to ensure is that your staff are given sufficient time in which to carry out the task effectively. Any opportunity to reflect properly on professional practice should be encouraged.

The future will bring more video conferencing. There will be an explosion in the means of access to knowledge and training. This will affect you both as a learner and a deliverer. It may change the way that INSET happens. But the most important thing is always the trainer and what he has to say. Judgements are made about you every time you stand up in front of your colleagues. Make sure that you do it well.

24 Dealing with staff attendance

Have a structured and transparent process. And use it

This is an extremely sensitive issue and is also one that is guaranteed to come your way eventually. The failure of some teachers to come to school not only ruins your day but also seriously inhibits learning. You will have to address it.

Whatever you are planning, a day will fall apart if you haven't enough teachers in the classroom. You might find yourself dashing from class to class, covering lessons and managing a developing crisis. You will want to put yourself in the front line and in so doing will achieve none of the things that you are paid to do. You need to think carefully about this. It is always easy to put yourself forward to cover three classes in the hall because staff are away, but is it really a productive use of your time? Or the head's? Only you can answer this.

Absence through illness also erodes staff morale. Your staff would like to think of themselves as a team. That belief is undermined when staff feel taken for a ride by their colleagues. They look at who is away and draw their own conclusions. They feel that difficulties are being shovelled onto the conscientious who turn up every day. Soon they too will crack. 'See I told you all along that it was a dodgy school. Look what it has done to you. Join the club.' They shouldn't always blame the leadership team, even though they do. It is their colleagues who are at fault. Ask around in every staffroom and the teachers will tell you who is always ready to pull a fast one. You must never avoid addressing this.

Every organization needs to deal with illness, but teaching is different because the work cannot be postponed. The class is there waiting to be taught. I can't put Year 9 in the pending tray to be dealt with tomorrow. They are there. And teachers get ratty. No one wants to take an extra lesson. Neither do you want to pay out money you can't afford from a tight budget on supply cover. Other important work isn't completed because of the need to get a body in front of a class. Strategic planning, staff development, all goes out of the window. A day can quickly become an exercise in crisis management. All you can do is to make sure the classes don't bite each other. But the really dramatic days when seven staff have gone down with flu aren't the issue. On these occasions everyone does come together. The fit staff rally round and award themselves campaign medals for bravery. No, it is the insidious accumulation of absence that bites, that steals time.

Everyone is busy. Everyone is doing something vital. Everyone believes that someone else should cover a class. But whether willing or not, someone has to do it. And when you look at the statistics, you will find that too many classes are supervised, not taught. Parents send their children to school for one thing and then we say we can't provide it. Students sit around. They do nothing. And another part of their education is wasted. Supply staff are indispensable but they can't always solve the issue of the early-morning phone call on the day when you already have three staff out on courses.

Long-term sickness can be managed more effectively. You can re-deploy staff within departments to maximize experience. Staff are always prepared to take on an extra lesson or two to preserve the examination classes. You can implement a structured response that minimizes the disruption. The real problems emerge with the unexpected absence, the head-cold, the stomach disorder.

The increasing sophistication of computer systems means that you should have all the data to hand that you need. You should review the data regularly and subject them to analysis. In this way you can easily see any patterns in staff attendance. You should also look at the statistics from a student's point of view. This can be a salutary experience when you see how many occasions some students are not taught by their designated teacher. If anything is designed to make you take action it is this. The school exists to provide a continuous meaningful education to the students. And when it starts to provide a fragmentary one then it fails.

It is a difficult issue but you cannot turn a blind eye to those staff with a poor attendance record. When you question teachers about their attendance record you are perceived as questioning their honesty. It is seen as an insult to their professionalism. They can be extremely defensive, and yet frequently contradictory. They will complain viciously about other staff being ill. No one should be absent. Everyone is malingering. Apart from themselves. When they are ill they are really ill. Theirs is the only absence that is genuine. An exaggeration of course, but never underestimate the feelings that fester when colleagues are away. The climate in employment is changing. The teacher who cannot be inspirational today because they are off colour still needs to attend school. We have no time for prima donnas. In fact, schools don't want the mercurial genius, the brilliant mind with the dodgy attendance. When you have been deputy head for a while you will be happy to settle for the average teacher who is there all the time. Sad perhaps, but true.

Your school is not a charity. They are places of employment. When a teacher signs on the dotted line they accept a raft of professional obligations along with the cash. And the foremost of these obligations is to turn up for work. You must keep this at the front of your mind. You will always be sympathetic to the teacher who has to deal with an unexpected domestic problem. When water starts coming through the ceiling in the middle of the night then Year 10 is unlikely to be in the forefront of your mind. When 3 year old Jessica is rushed into hospital with suspected meningitis you will not expect her mother to leave the bedside in order to teach GCSE history. But at the same time, it is not the school's duty to resolve repeated childcare issues. If a teacher wants full-time pay then they must accept all the obligations that go with it. Picking up little Simon everyday at noon is their problem, not yours.

You should have a clearly defined policy for managing the issue of staff attendance. The first thing you will have in place will be the return-to-work interview. Some colleagues might be affronted that they are questioned, but this is sound practice. 'How are you? Is there anything I can do?' It doesn't really need to be more than that, though it depends of course upon why they have been away.

Your policy should include specific trigger points about which everyone is aware. When a teacher has accrued a specific amount of absence or appears to experience repeated illness or develops a pattern, then you need to explore the reasons. Why is it happening? Is there an institutional reason? Is there a class that is being avoided? Or an individual or a responsibility?

The majority of your staff will not want to be away from school. They will feel an obligation to the children they teach and do not require a robust absence management policy to make them attend. But you will have individuals to deal with. The quota man lives and breathes in many schools. 'You give me six covers and I'll have a stomach bug for a day. It's payback time.' There can be a suspicious illness before or immediately after holidays, usually the result of inconveniently timed flights.

We need to look at what is causing poor attendance and offer support where we can. But we should not be afraid of disciplinary action when necessary because the whole school suffers when teachers don't turn up for work. These things might be painful to confront but they do happen and staff are quick to spot it. They are also quick to spot that you are avoiding it. When you feel it is appropriate, choose a time and a venue you are comfortable with, marshal your evidence and plan what you are going to say, writing it down if you need to. Be ready for the fact that staff are likely to deny it and to be affronted. But if you get to this stage you will have documentary evidence to support you, for this is how you have discerned a pattern. I once spoke to a colleague about the fact that they had missed the first Monday in December for six successive years. I had evidence. I never found out why but it didn't happen again.

Formal proceedings can happen quite quickly if there is no improve-ment in a teacher's attendance. This can have catastrophic consequences for a younger teacher. Once a meeting takes place it becomes a fact. That meeting did take place and is documented. As such it will feature in references. Who wants to appoint a teacher with a dodgy attendance record? You must remind your staff of this painful fact. If they don't like it that much in your school, a high rate of absence means that no other school will touch them and they will never get out of it.

25 Innovate!

Give yourself time to think

Something that is clear is that having the inspiration for an adaptation or innovation is just a part of any change you are implementing. You need to have the energy and the attention to detail to see it through. Too often in schools, and your colleagues may remind you of this in a teacher's typically cynical manner, ideas are introduced with a flourish and then are allowed to fade. Their long-term impact may be negligible. Often this is because other things come along that get in the way. Schools have always been rampant with change, to the extent that innovation fatigue sets in. Teachers snort with derision at the new scheme thrown up on the flip chart. Another new idea, another initiative, championed by someone with a hungry promotion to feed. Teachers are notoriously dismissive. The best deputy head is one who steps outside this stereotype, who ensures that their school is not destabilized by unnecessary change.

There is a great deal to be said for a measured approach, one that always remains in contact with the unchanging principles of secondary school education. Any change must not be a risk designed to aid career enhancement. It must be a change designed to enhance pupil achievement. Of course many are resistant to change and will oppose any idea at all. You have to be courageous and not allow yourself to be deflected from what you perceive is the true path by the cynical voices from the worn armchairs. You must be confident in your own judgement and have the energy to see your ideas through. If it is worth doing, then it must be worth doing properly. And of course you must give yourself time and space in which you can develop new ideas. Don't overburden yourself with mundane tasks. Your job is far too important for that. Give yourself time for reflection and planning.

26 Cover

Don't be a martyr

Physically doing the cover may not be your job. Your opportunity to do so could happen automatically, generated by the computer. It could be the task of a senior member of staff. But no matter who puts it on the staffroom notice board you must be ready to take responsibility.

No one likes cover. It is seen as an intrusion, as a management conspiracy designed to ruin your day. This is especially the case if the cover is for a member of the leadership team who is on a course or at a meeting. It is a sure-fire way of making sure that the head's name is mud if someone else has to cover for them. You will be no different to anyone else. You won't like it much either. But never let anyone hear you complain about it. An unguarded comment can be all that is needed for a split to be perceived within the leadership team. Never ally yourself with those who complain. You must stand squarely with the person who sorts it out.

What staff conveniently forget is that cover is not a management creation. It is a response to a circumstance that is beyond leadership control – and that is staff phoning in ill. Even in these days of workload agreements, cover still generates lots of bile and unhappiness. Your own position is also protected by the agreement, so don't do more cover than you need to. Covering every lesson under the sun will certainly earn you brownie points. Your colleagues will be happy to let you do this. You will be a real hero. But it will definitely stop you doing the job you are paid to do. You will be reducing yourself to the level of a supply teacher.

Naturally there will be occasions where you have to be seen to be leading from the front, taking on an extra burden in exceptional circumstances. This, however, can't go on forever. You are paid to make difficult decisions and the difficult decision might well be not to do cover yourself because you have something more important to do. Avoid getting bogged down in this sort of institutional maintenance.

Obviously the cover list and the statistics it generates needs to be accessible and transparent. You must be able to defend the decisions that have been made about others' and your own record. The nature of the classes covered should also be noted. Are difficult classes distributed fairly or does the burden fall too often upon certain teachers? Always be aware of what is going on in the cover list because some colleagues in the staffroom will analyse it in minute detail.

It is important to retain the confidentiality of the cover list as much as you can. Some students will use prior knowledge of a cover list to inform their truancy plans. Even within the framework that legislation has established, there will be tensions and complaints. What you must do at times is to ask yourself why is cover happening. Is there a pattern forming that you need to address?

Cover can be generated by an excessive enthusiasm for INSET. Suddenly, in your desire for school improvement, your school may be marginalizing the needs of classes. The teacher who they need to teach them is locked into observations and meetings. Think about this. Is release from lessons really the most productive way of achieving your objectives? Is it worth the disruption? If it isn't, find some other way of achieving them. Twilight sessions and weekend workshops can often be equally productive and do not disrupt the school in the same way. In these days of flexible employment regulations it might in fact be better to pay your staff for such work in their own time, rather than to generate cover lessons. This is of course an aspect of cover that you can control. You can, in moments of difficulty, stop teachers going on a course. You won't be popular but the daily needs of the students in the school must be the priority.

If you find that the cover list illustrates concerns you have about staff attendance, then you have a different problem altogether.

27 Holding management meetings

You can't manage a school from a classroom

Of course you need to hold management meetings. The question is when? Certainly you need to meet every day before the opening of business. What is happening today? Who is coming? What happened yesterday? It is the only way to keep everyone efficiently well-informed. They are an integral part of managing a complex organism like a school. An informal exchange of information. But you will also need to have more formal meetings.

Why shouldn't you hold them during the school day? After all, you are running a big budget, influencing the destiny of hundreds of people. Why should you do this after school? It also means that you can attend other meetings like departmental ones after school. Staff, however, may resent this. They will not like you making yourself inaccessible during working hours. Some staff will try to subvert it, always phoning, always finding a crisis. This is because they believe that you exist only to serve their needs. You are really lucky to be outside the classroom, it's not fair. You must pay for your position. We must stay after school for meetings. So should you. But life is never so straightforward. You have every right to hold meetings during the course of the day. It is the professional thing to do. Teachers are big boys and girls. They need to respect the different nature of your job. They'd have plenty to say if the school went bankrupt.

Naturally your meetings have to be more than just casual gossips and the danger is that the longer the team is together that is what they can become. Always insist upon an agenda and a structure. Some meetings should concentrate on single issues like dyslexia or primary liaison. Others could take the form of a report back to the team from the different areas of responsibility or from an important INSET course or visit. You can invite other members of staff to discuss different issues or interesting developments in their subject.

Meetings should be properly chaired and minutes taken. I would think that they should be made accessible to the governing body on request, but they should not, as a matter of course, be made available to teaching staff. This could have the effect of inhibiting discussion. Confidentiality is important and the team needs to feel relaxed in the forum if you are all going to do your job properly. The meetings will serve to bond the team together and help a new team develop trust. You don't have to like each other, though it helps, but you must be able to trust each other.

28 Maintaining effective primary liaison

Education must be part of a continuum

As with many things it is always a good idea to examine your purposes. What is it about? What is it for? Who is it for? To answer the last question first, then it should be obvious that primary liaison exists for the students themselves. Successfully established and operated, it should ease their passage into a new phase in their education. But it is never that simple. It can also help teachers working in both Key Stages. It can broaden perspectives and improve the quality of lessons delivered. It can also help significantly in marketing your school – which is really important if you are having problems maintaining student numbers. It becomes an area which you should never ignore.

It is obvious that you need to provide an important link between your school and partner schools that provide the students. It is about being a professional. You need to know about your raw material. You have a duty to do this so that there is some kind of continuity and progression between Key Stages. Teachers need to be aware of prior knowledge so that they can build upon it. There should be a mechanism for this sort of curriculum coordination through subject-based working parties. Primary schools need to know what their children can expect, to know what topics are covered and what sort of experiences are useful for them to have had. In your own school you will need to coordinate in some way all the different experiences that students from a mixture of schools can bring with them. Your English department could be seriously miffed if they discover one of the partner schools teaches the book that is the basis of the Year 7 scheme of work.

Such working parties are very valuable in developing knowledge and for acting as a catalyst for discussion and research. Don't forget that your school is an important thing that all your partner schools have in common and it means that you can serve a useful professional purpose by offering a venue and an occasion for meetings. You also have specialist staff and facilities that primary schools can use. It might cost you very little but it could really help the Year 6 curriculum. You have specialist areas like technology suites, extensive art facilities, networked computer rooms that you should try to share. This is all part of establishing education as a continuum. If you are fortunate to have these facilities in your school then you have a responsibility to allow the community to exploit them.

Teachers need to talk and to understand each other. Secondary teachers are often amazed at the standard of work in primary schools. They can be surprised at the sort of skills acquired by students and the depth of understanding displayed. It does say something about what often happens in the early years in secondary education that teachers are often surprised when they compare the high standard of Year 6 work with that completed in Year 7. As deputy you would be well advised to examine this as a project with a working party from both Key Stages. It is a good way of drawing staff together and promoting student achievement.

Always listen to your primary partners. They will have worked with Year 6 very closely and will have forged important and lasting relationships. They will want to feel that the oldest students in their school are going to settle in and take every opportunity presented to them. The fact that their teacher has links to the big school will be important to them. They will inevitably lose status when they transfer. Suddenly, instead of being the oldest in a small school, trusted and with responsibility, they will become the smallest fish in a pond full of sharks. To know that their teacher is part of the process, and will be informed of their progress, is vital. They can promote an awareness of all the exciting things they will do and such expectations will carry students through the early disorientating days.

Coming to secondary school isn't a break with the past. It is merely a new arena in which to display your talents. In this way, realistic expectations can be passed on to new teachers. It might prevent able students taking things just a bit too easy in the early days because they feel anonymous and unrecognized. This is important, especially since liaison is traditionally more thorough when it involves students with learning difficulties. You need to be able to tell your staff about talents and achievements as well as illnesses and conditions. You need to make yourself aware of any particular learning or physical challenges that your new students might face. This may require you to research particular conditions and to lead your staff to an understanding of their implications.

Of course, you might need to establish the impression that coming to your school is the natural course of events for students from your partners. In these competitive days once students start drifting to other schools and your numbers decline you could be facing all kinds of problems. You will have to lose staff and you will probably find that the profile of your intake starts to change. When you lose students it is almost always the more able ones who go first. Any event involving primary teachers is a very important one. You need to ensure that the school is presenting itself at its best, with good displays and quality work. Make sure that staff who meet with their colleagues from partner schools actually know their names. Primary teachers are very influential people. They meet parents regularly and can pass on impressions as well as information. This can be especially important on those occasions when you receive negative publicity. It happens to all of us at one time or another, and if you have someone putting a story into some sort of context it can be a big help.

If we are talking about liaison being a continuum, then the first few days of a new school career are part of it too. You will need to familiarize the children with the school and its layout; the spaces and the faces. There is, however, a limit to what you should do. In the end they must learn to swim in this new pool without armbands. You do not want the excitement they feel on coming to a new school to be dissipated by extended induction sessions.

You need to get them into classrooms and learning something new. You need to build upon their eagerness and set a learning agenda. Introduce them to their form tutor and other significant people, give them a timetable and get them learning. It has always seemed to me better to do their introduction to the ways of the school gradually over a number of days. Get them into lessons. Don't put them into a Year 7 ghetto to bond together and form new friendships across their primary schools. They will do this themselves very efficiently. As an activity this may also generate levels of cover that could in turn set off the new year for other year groups on the wrong foot completely.

Your own role as deputy head and your seniority may not be recognized or understood by new students in the school. But they will learn because of the way you present yourself to them in assembly and around the school.

Soon they will become acclimatized. Some will find it harder than others. Some will find the work easy. Some will find it hard to handle cash and to manage their day on their own. Others will regret their loss of status as the seniors in their school. But change is inevitable. It needs to be embraced and managed by us all, not just transitional students. The chances are that complaints or concerns of parents will come straight to you since that is the model in many primary schools. Parents go straight to the class teacher and often straight to the head. Don't be surprised if in the first few months you are taking calls about PE kit and dinner money. But always be patient and deal with things with patience and sympathy. This is how your school is marketed. Through impressions formed and spread by word of mouth. Your manner is representative of your school – and word gets around.

Never forget that it is the parents who make the decision about which school their children attend. You can put on a wonderful show for the students when they visit the school, but it will make no difference if you don't manage to convince their parents. They need to believe that coming to your school is the natural and automatic choice. It is up to you to make that happen.

29 Managing behaviour

Avoid getting involved too soon

When you first arrive in the school it is important that you get a feel of the tone of the place. Walk the corridors during lessons and between them. This is always highly revealing. Do corridor duty with another member of the leadership team. It is good to work together since it will establish in the students' minds that you are part of a genuine team. You can be introduced to pupils and get a sense of how issues are dealt with. All too soon they will accept you as part of their daily landscape. Establishing yourself in this way isn't that difficult to do. It is when you start to deal with issues on behalf of other professionals that things start to get more complex.

You will inevitably be seen as someone who has the answers. Whether you feel confident in this area or not, it is something that you will have to manage. On appointment as a deputy head you will have already developed ways of managing difficult situations. You wouldn't have been given the job if you hadn't already shown that facility. What will happen is that you will now see these issues in a wider context. Instead of dealing with behaviour in a clearly defined area, you will now be dealing with it across the school as a whole. You will see some interesting things.

When you step back and observe how teachers behave in challenging situations, you will see how some teachers can, through their reactions, make things so much worse. They are people too and they can make mistakes. They can inflame situations because they become emotionally involved or injured. This is what happens in the classroom. Teachers need to react to situations with their heads not their emotions. They have to remember that they are professionals. This of course can be very difficult when dealing with a difficult class, because their behaviour appears like an assault upon the teacher's own personality and everything that they hold dear. They become possessed by anger, fear and impotence. In the classroom everything is personal. It is no wonder stress levels in the teaching profession are so high. At moments like these they will turn to you for support and reassurance. Perhaps they will feel unable to deal with a problem themselves. Perhaps they don't want to. Either way you will have to deal with it.

The first thing you must always do is support your staff. That should never be in question. Whatever has happened, your first response must be to defuse and support. If you think that the teacher has got it wrong, then share that with them later, privately and certainly not in front of students. Do it when there has been an opportunity for reflection. The fact that everything needs to be written down helps in these circum-stances, since an incident report imposes a shape on events and implies some sort of simple analysis. Always insist on a written report, unless of course there has been a major drama that requires your immediate involvement. Under the *Freedom of Information Act 2005* such reports may have to be revealed, and so all files need to be ordered, accessible and up-to-date.

Don't forget, whatever happens staff will generally blame you. If you ran the school better, if you expelled Natasha, if you spent all day patrolling the corridors, then these things wouldn't happen. You are paid more, you sort it out.

What you need is an agreed staged referral process that should, in theory, ensure that disciplinary responses are proportionate. From classroom teacher, to head of department and then on through the pastoral system. The idea is that you will not be involved too soon, that you and the head retain some distance and gravity so that students realize how serious something is once you get involved. You need to have a policy that is understood by students, their parents and the teachers.

The staff will try always to circumvent it. They might use personal contact or rely upon you to do them favours. And it is difficult, if Marie is always bailing you out with file paper and sharing her worksheets, not to want to help when Jamie writes all over a table. But on the whole you should not be dealing with these situations. You need to be dealing with accumulations, with patterns, when other staff have already had their say. You should be part of a gradual process of escalation. It is not unusual for a member of staff to send to you directly for help and, whatever procedures you have established, you have to respond. Your reputation depends upon it. You can never refuse. You can speak to a teacher afterwards and remind them of established procedures, but when called you have no choice. How you handle the situation – your speed of response, your effectiveness, your retribution – will influence how others see you, especially in the early days of your tenure.

Generally speaking, managing student behaviour isn't about behaviour at all. Of course, there are students who display very challenging behaviour, who are disturbed or maladjusted. But often the issue of student behaviour is just another expression of staffroom and school politics.

When you are called to an issue of general classroom disruption you need to achieve order pretty quickly. Often the best way is by remaining calm and by standing silently at the front of the disruptive class. They will recognize the dynamics of the situation. You have been called to their classroom and your introduction should break the spell of unreason. If you do need to offer the teacher advice on classroom management, then this is clearly the wrong time to do so. Express your disappointment and apologize to the member of staff on behalf of the class and indicate what they will do by means of reparation. You are thus establishing yourself as their representative. This is important, because you are then speaking about their failings publicly and implying that you are going to work together to resolve issues. You are sorry that they have let themselves – and you – down. You speak to the teacher on behalf of the class and you may then address the teacher privately if you need to. Take away any significant problem students and deal with them in your own space. Make them uncomfortable by waiting for your attention. Continue with your own paperwork whilst they wait. This indicates that you are an important person who has other things to deal with. They need to know that they have stepped up a level as a result of misbehaviour. Don't hesitate to use the computer to obtain a telephone number. It sends out a message that you are in possession of information about them, and knowledge is power.

Of course, an explosion of righteous anger has its place too. Bursting angrily into a classroom can certainly be dramatic, but the problem with anger is that it can lead to incoherence and it is undignified to struggle for words at a moment when you really need to show that you are in control. If you don't go apoplectic very often and the students know this, it can be extremely effective, but never overplay your hand or its dramatic effect will lose its edge.

When you are called on, never forget that the class has won. They have prevented learning taking place, putting in its place the thrill of subverting authority, of revenge on the system. And what the class or student will know, even if they cannot articulate it properly, is that they have chipped away at the teacher's status. The message they are transmitting is, 'We will behave for you. But we won't behave for them.' This is not likely to fill the teacher with self-confidence. Always report back to the member of staff about what you have done and how you are going to monitor the situation in order to try to ensure it won't happen again. This might enable you to meet with a member of staff who is experiencing more difficulty than you would anticipate.

If students manipulate disruption then so do teachers. Never believe for a moment that you are in control of classroom situations. You are not. The politics of the school are much more twisted and murky than that. You will be manipulated and sometimes there will be nothing that you can do about it. For example: a member of staff has an option group in Year 10 that contains two students they don't want. They are disrespectful and disruptive. The teacher wants them out. You say no. The students chose the subject, for whatever reason, as they were entitled to do. To take them out means that they will be put in a class which they haven't chosen. A problem will be passed on to another colleague. All this makes perfect sense, but it still leaves the teacher with a difficult situation to manage in their classroom. The teacher therefore manipulates the situation. They will make the lessons so difficult for the students that they eventually ask to move themselves, or they become, in response, so disruptive that they seriously undermine the chances of others in the class. Suddenly you are dealing with an issue you never wanted to deal with.

It can happen too where staff want to drive out low-ability students who might affect their pass rate into a different subject 'more suited to them'. When you have to deal with such occasions your wish to support the aspirations of your students will have been undermined. You will be left with no choices. By all means speak to the staff concerned to express your displeasure. But what are you going to do with the students? They don't want to go back into a subject where they have been made to feel terminally unwelcome. To put them back in will give you more headaches later. Game, set and match.

It is important that you don't get offences against yourself out of proportion. You must always be seen to be acting consistently. If a student upsets you there are a number of things you need to bear in mind. In the first place, it is a challenge to the political structure of the school. You can't ignore an incident that involves you, even if you wanted to. The students realize that you have some sort of seniority so if they wish to strike against the system it wouldn't be unusual for them to target you. If something happens that you are inclined to shrug off, then always be aware that, because of who you are, you might be unleashing the forces of misrule if you do so. If it isn't an assault on you as a teacher, it might in fact be an assault on what you represent. I have never had a problem with being sworn at. A barely audible slurry of abuse doesn't touch me at all. It never has. But as a deputy I can never ignore it.

At the same time, you need to be consistent. Your staffroom reputation will be in tatters if you take more seriously incidents involving yourself and trivialize similar incidents involving a head of department. Don't send them for additional language support when they swear at the head of technology and the boil them in oil when they swear at you.

Managing behaviour? It is never simple. Because it is politics.

30 Excluding students

Every exclusion represents a failure. Make sure it is not a failure of your school

It is inevitable that exclusion will become a huge issue that will suck you in at some time during your career as part of a leadership team. You will be unable to avoid it and the sadness is that you will spend a great deal of time doing something that is essentially negative. It is also fraught with difficulties and has gathered around itself a considerable volume of law. This is designed to prevent any infringement of an individual's human rights by denying them a right to an education. What this means is that you must approach this emotive issue with a great deal of care.

It is very easy for schools to act in haste and in anger and this can lead them into really significant difficulties if they do not take account of the legal implications of what they do. School exclusions very quickly become the focus of legal proceedings and if you have got even a small detail wrong, then your entire position could collapse. You could find yourself having to face your staff and tell them that you got it wrong and, more importantly, that the student concerned is back in their classroom.

There is a real tension at the centre of the issue. Your staff will contain within it some who believe that everyone should be excluded for everything. At the same time, out of schools there is a significant body of opinion that believes exclusion shouldn't be happening at all.

For a number of obvious reasons there is an emphasis in government policy for inclusion, to keep all pupils in school as much as possible. As a result the acceptable criteria are restricted. You can't exclude for minor incidents, such as a failure to complete homework or poor academic progress, lateness or pregnancy. There is also a restriction that tries to prevent schools encouraging parents to keep their child at home as a way of dealing with troublesome behaviour or to avoid permanent exclusion. So if you observe what is going on, you will see schools anxious to promote the right messages in order to maintain pupil numbers. They will establish themselves as places with a strict division between right and wrong, where parents can see old-fashioned values still at work. You will also see that the professional associations are keen to protect their members from threats and abuse. So, not only will you have to manage troubled and difficult young people who have their own rights, and their parents, but also the politics of the staffroom.

If you look at what effect exclusions have, you will probably come to the conclusion that for many individual students they don't really work. But what teachers see is the part one student can play in a class and the influence they have, and they see the effects upon themselves. Facing the disengaged and the abusive on a daily basis is never easy. And why should teachers feel threatened when they go to work? However professional we try to be, we can all feel the need for revenge after pain or humiliation. Sometimes an exclusion can keep a hurt or offended teacher in school, because it brings with it a sense of finality, a sense that the incident has been dealt with and that the school and the teacher have won. It can be better than having a teacher phone in sick.

You will also know that the staff will pull together to support one of their own. In this way exclusion becomes a challenge to the leadership of the school, particularly since it provokes deeply held and entrenched views. 'Show that you support your staff by excluding the pupil. If you don't exclude, then it is clear that you do not support your staff.' Obviously if teachers feel unsupported and isolated, then there will be more confrontations.

It is also an issue in which you can be easily manipulated by the staff. Whatever sorts of procedures you may have for the sort of staged referral system referred to in the previous section, there will still be colleagues who do their best to circumvent it. There is clear evidence that when established procedures for dealing with behaviour are avoided and pupils are sent directly to senior staff, then they are more likely to be excluded immediately. The headteacher knows that the professional associations can threaten to strike if they feel that exclusions are not used in support of teachers. Suddenly there is no room for manoeuvre. If a pupil swears and the teacher announces to the class that they will thus be excluded, what options do you have? You can speak to that person and tell them not to put you in that position again, but on that particular occasion you have little choice. You can't let the students see that you believe a teacher is wrong and has perhaps mishandled an incident. Suddenly, the potentially excluded pupil can become a pawn in the murky chess game of the staffroom.

What you have to do is to examine the frequency of such incidents. Is there a pattern emerging that indicates either that the teacher is not coping or perhaps suggests how they are viewing you. Are they avoiding their responsibilities? Or are they trying in fact to undermine you? They may have no respect for you and may be suggesting that all the difficulties in the school are your fault. Are they putting you in a difficult position in the hope that you do in fact get it wrong, so that they can have a go at you in the staffroom. All staffrooms are nests of gossip. It is what keeps some teachers going.

As a leadership team, you have to promote good behaviour and discipline and secure an orderly and safe environment. You should respond to inappropriate behaviour within the context of the school's behaviour policy and this should have a range of strategies in it, with exclusion as one option. Alternative punitive sanctions can be suggested, such as exclusion from a class rather than school, to be supervised by another teacher, perhaps in some sort of 'sin bin' provision. Such arrangements can breed resentment. They are expensive to run and teachers do not regard staffing them as an exciting prospect. It can call upon a great deal of time from the leadership of the school to ensure their success, which is not necessarily cost-effective. You are not paid to act as some sort of jailer, so there should be no obligation upon the leadership team to staff such a provision permanently. You have better things to do. This is not leadership. And you might not be especially good at it anyway.

You can always seek help from behaviour specialists, but anyone from outside the school is obviously not perceived as a full-time member of staff. If they are there to offer advice then often that advice, however good it might be, is not accepted because they do not seem to work under the same institutional pressures. If you are looking to develop expertise, then it can be more effective if you can nurture talent within the school to offer support to others.

One of the enduring myths about exclusion is that it can only be exacted for misdemeanours within school. Out-of-school behaviour can lead to exclusion too. The abuse of teachers in public is an obvious example where schools are keen to act. Again, it is part of the way in which you support your staff as professionals and of how you are perceived.

Other serious incidents that happen in the community could indeed be regarded as an affront to school values and reputation and necessitate a response from you. However, schools must be very careful to ensure that their reactions are not regarded as prejudging an issue where there may eventually be criminal proceedings. This can be especially difficult where the victim and the alleged aggressor are both in your school. Their parents can't be expected to assess the position logically and dispassionately. They will be demanding school support for their own child. Stay out of it if you can. Rape accusations can prove to be a particularly difficult issue, because of the danger of making prejudicial decisions. You may exclude the boy in order to ensure good order in the school but are you saying that he is inevitably guilty? And if you exclude the girl to protect her from rumour and pressure from others to retract an accusation, are you then saying that she has made it all up? In such circumstances it is important to seek appropriate advice.

Whenever you are dealing with an incident in school, you will have to question students about it. Obviously you should take any statements as soon as possible after an incident. Natural justice suggests that pupils should be given every opportunity to give their version of events. Only those who directly witnessed an incident should be asked to provide a statement. Pupils should not be asked leading questions. Questioning of pupils is a particularly sensitive issue. Never try to emulate fictional TV detectives attempting to catch out master criminals through clever questions and sophisticated wordplay. It is not your job. Whilst it was established in law in 1997 that teachers are not bound by the same code of conduct as the police in questioning pupils, the fact remains that you need to exercise some caution.

The searching of pupils is ill-advised, no matter what suspicions you might harbour. You may search a desk or a locker because that is the property of the school, but not a school bag because that belongs to someone else. You may ask a pupil to empty out their pockets, but they are not obliged to do so. A body search without consent would be regarded as an assault.

A pupil must be given a fair hearing and they and their parents must know the nature of any accusations being made. This is particularly important with regard to permanent exclusion procedures. Always write things down, for any part of an incident could come back to haunt you if you haven't done it properly.

What you will find, usually, is that more boys are excluded than girls. Government statistics are quite clear on this and show that the highest proportion come from the 13–15 year old age group and many of them carry with them statements of special educational needs. Look at the pattern as it emerges in your own school, because there are lessons to be learned about how your school is functioning and how some situations are being managed.

It is clear that boys and girls tend to sort out problems between themselves in different ways. Girls often sort out disagreements verbally. They argue, they talk things through. Sometimes teachers become involved, but generally they sort things out for themselves. Boys, on the other hand, can often sort out issues physically by fighting or through threats. They are concerned to keep face amongst their peers, to maintain a reputation and their social standing. This leads inevitably to conflict with a school, an institution that tries to hold such issues in check. This leads to exclusions.

There are generally two official reasons why students are excluded. One is 'threatening others with intended or actual physical harm' which encompasses bullying. The other is a persistent refusal to conform to the purposes of the classroom, which is generally disruptive behaviour. You might find yourself that the majority of exclusions are for the verbal abuse of school staff.

The majority of students regard exclusion as a very severe sanction indeed, the ultimate punishment. It is akin to being thrown out of the family, carrying with it a sense of rejection. If it happened to them they would be mortified, for they have the sophistication to realize that they have offended against the community they want to be a part of and so care about their rejection. Others though can regard exclusion as a badge of honour. And if you do not like school very much, then you can get an extra holiday by swearing at a teacher, preferably a senior member of staff. For some it is a price worth paying. Parents themselves often react with confusion and anger when an exclusion happens. They cannot always understand how what they see as extra days off can be regarded as a punishment. The fact that their child's right to continuity of education has been taken away from them can also provoke resentment.

You need to remember that the risks associated with exclusion are huge. In the end, statistics indicate that excluded pupils are more likely to face unemployment or homelessness. In addition, they are more likely to become involved in crime. So remember, you mustn't rush into an exclusion just to get brownie points from the staffroom. You have a responsibility to consider the wider consequences. An exclusion is not a triumph. It indicates that something has gone wrong. And the existence of repeat offenders suggests that it doesn't always work; however, day to day experience means that you have to embrace it as a necessary evil, as a quick fix. It has to exist as the ultimate sanction.

A permanent exclusion is a ritual washing of hands. A school has done all it can with a troubled or difficult pupil. Now it must cast them out, to become someone else's problem. Normally it is used only as a last resort, when a range of other strategies has been exhausted. For a serious incident, though, the option remains to permanently exclude for a first offence. Sexual misconduct, drugs offences and incidents involving an offensive weapon are the sort of things that can provoke it.

The LEA must make arrangements as best they can to continue the pupil's education. The problem they must face is the natural reluctance that another school might feel in adopting someone else's problem pupil. Sometimes the student will have been chastened by the experience and a change of institution is a positive step. On other occasions though the old problems quickly emerge. And a leadership team, aware of how the wider school community may react, would have to think very carefully before they take on a student who has been excluded elsewhere. If the staff in the school are not open-minded in giving someone another chance then a new crisis can be provoked quickly. But again, as a deputy, you must be aware of your wider responsibility to be ready to give someone another chance. What happens to those you permanently exclude? Colleagues in other schools have to pick them up eventually. So if you want others to work with you, you must be ready to work with them.

31 Dealing with bullying

Never ignore or trivialize

Bullying is quite rightly a high-profile issue. Everyone has been to
school and believes that confers upon them the status of an expert.
Many have witnessed bullying in some form or other. No one wants
to think that their own child might be a victim. The consequences
might be too great to bear – with long-term damage to self-respect and
confidence from which some never recover. You would certainly be
horrified if you discovered that your school had a reputation for not
dealing with bullying properly. There are schools, as you probably
know, that have tragic stories to tell.

To what extent it is a reflection of human nature I am not in a
position to say, but you can be confident that bullying in the student
body in some form will come your way. It seems to me that there are
those who feel the need to establish the sort of pecking order that exists
amongst chickens. It is important to them that they are aware of where
they are in relation to others. They need someone to pick on to make
themselves feel good. It is not the place of this book to explore the
issue in great detail. Others have written with far greater awareness and
understanding, and the body of literature available is extensive. But
bullies are not well-rounded individuals.

You need to make sure that your school has a visible and working
anti-bullying policy. This may need to reflect an LEA perspective.
It must be available to all and students and parents need to be aware of
its contents and its implementation. At their most effective, anti-
bullying strategies involve the students themselves. They will carry far

greater weight if students are involved in their development
and implementation.

The use of mentors who make themselves available can be very
useful. These are often older students who might be easier to approach
than teachers. It may be especially useful if you can recruit students
who themselves may have been victims of long- or short-term bullying.
They then carry with them a credibility that a teacher could not match.
You might need to consider training for students who want to be
mentors. This is often very successful, for it gives the mentors status and
a sense of worth and achievement. They can establish drop-in centres,
buddying, paired reading and a private listening space. You can establish
bully boxes where victims can make the first approach for help. A raised
profile for bullying through assemblies is always a good idea. External
organizations may too wish to be involved and have something
important to offer.

It is not necessarily your responsibility to coordinate all the resources
available. There may be others in the school who would be better
placed to do so. But in your position you will be expected to act with
calm assurance and with a confident grasp of what is right and wrong.
People will expect you to sort it out. Distressed parents and intimidated
students will expect retribution. It is never that straightforward.

One of the first things that needs to be done is to untangle a web
of relationships that has led to the bullying being revealed. It shouldn't
really be your job to do this. Others, like heads of year and heads of
school, should have a much more informed awareness of the dynamics
amongst their students. You may be drawn into it, but largely you need
to leave the detailed investigations to others. Your job is to formulate
judgements and to offer leadership. You need to show that this is an
issue that you take seriously, so seriously in fact that you allow it to
impact upon your own important work as a manager of the school.

There is a difficulty here, however. In order to establish the facts of
a case an investigation must be carried out. Natural justice would say
that this is essential. However, the nature of the investigation might
suggest to the victim that you don't believe them. The aggressor has
to receive an audience and they will usually trivialize the issue, saying
that they were only joking or teasing. The victim is just hypersensitive
and has misunderstood bog-standard horseplay. In this process, both
sides are given equal weight and the assaults are thus balanced against
the victim's actions and reactions. This merely acts to convince the

victim that they are somehow guilty, that they have done something
wrong. As a result, to the victim, who feels emotionally vulnerable
anyway, any investigation can seem accusatory, adding to their sense of
worthlessness. They can think that what has happened is an inevitable
result of their own failings. So you need to make sure that your staff
work very hard to explain the justice of the procedure and the way
that it will lead to an informed and accurate judgement. Still, there is
no room for any doubt. You all have to show that you are on the side
of the bullied.

Never forget, however, that just because someone says they are being
bullied, it doesn't mean that they are. Often it is an umbrella term for
anxiety – and that could have many causes. Parents are particularly keen
to trot out suggestions of bullying because they believe that it puts you
on the back foot. Such false accusations need to be met robustly, since
they trivialize the pain of those who are genuine bullying victims.

It may seem inappropriate at times but don't forget that the bully
may need help too. They are displaying aberrant behaviour so they are
likely to have issues of their own to deal with. Excluding them from
school is an understandable act of revenge by a disapproving community,
but it may not be the means by which you can stop the bullying. As
with all exclusions, never act in haste. If you do, you are quite likely
to get it wrong. You may be put under pressure by staff and parents to
exact immediate retribution. You can understand this. No one wants
a child to be bullied and everyone wants to feel that they can offer
protection. But in any case of bullying, there is normally more than one
victim. One is usually the bully. You have a responsibility to both of
them. The school needs to work with all of its pupils. All have their
rights and the school has an obligation to prepare them for constructive
adult life within an acceptable moral framework. It is important that all
students are encouraged to reflect upon their behaviour. Counselling
and punishment must be linked, to indicate that some actions are
unacceptable within a framework of moral absolutes, not only because
the victim is different or weak or inadequate. All our lives must be
linked to essential concepts of right and wrong.

So whilst you may have an instinctive urge to support and protect
the victim, never deny yourself that valuable moment for reflection
about all of your responsibilities.

32 Managing medical needs

Keep informed

At the time of writing, concerns about administering medication to pupils represent one of the most common enquiries received by teacher unions. Medication in school is no longer just an occasional spoonful of amoxycilin. Now ailments such as asthma, epilepsy and diabetes have been joined by anaphylaxis – an extreme allergic reaction to foods such as nuts or dairy products. There are increased incidences of AIDS/HIV and hepatitis strains in schools. Tropical diseases are not unknown.

   The policy of inclusion means that there are many more children with medical needs in mainstream schools. You need to know what they are and what the school should do. The prime responsibility for a child's health rests with the parents or guardians and a teacher in your school can only act in response to their wishes. Parental responsibility includes the obligation to pass on appropriate information. If the school doesn't know about something then it can hardly be blamed for not acting in a supportive way. A parent can request of the headteacher that medication should be administered. The school staff should then be consulted and asked to volunteer. But at present there is no legal duty on them to do it. Giving medication or supervising a pupil taking it is not included in a teacher's conditions of employment. This is entirely a voluntary role. Any staff who do volunteer have a right to expect support, information and most importantly training. It is always particularly important to understand any side effects to any medication and what to do if they occur.

A school nurse's contract would obviously include such a responsibility, as would the contract of a dedicated support assistant who works with a specific child. However, no one – and that includes you – should feel pressurized into accepting the responsibility of administering medicines. If they feel uneasy and can support their reservations, then they should refuse. Their decision is defensible as long as it is clear that they have acted reasonably.

A particular circumstance that would require caution would be when the timing of the medication is of vital importance. Can a school always guarantee that it would be administered precisely? What about a situation where intimate contact would be required? As in so many situations, if in any sort of doubt you need to take professional advice. But also remember that schools must take reasonable practical steps to accommodate a pupil's medical needs. You can't simply turn them away. Of course, you need to be confident that the nature of any treatment needed is not incompatible with the education of other pupils in the school. On this basis, a school could refuse admission. You would have to be clear in the reasons for your decision.

The basic outline of a school response to medical needs falls within the scope of its health and safety policy. The employer, usually the LEA or the governing body, is legally obliged to maintain and review the policy, the headteacher is obliged to implement it. The policy exists to clarify the roles and responsibilities of staff, to offer reassurance and guidelines and to enable regular school attendance for all pupils. This is at the heart of the issues surrounding medical needs. It is part of a policy of inclusion. And if pupils with either long- or short-term medical needs are to be included, then the important thing is knowledge.

One of your responsibilities is to ensure that information is shared. All staff need to be aware of the precise nature of a condition. The details need to come from parents and health professionals. Staff in all the different parts of the school need to be aware of how likely an emergency is and what to do if one should occur. Common sense indicates that if a child has a specific support worker then back-up cover should be available in the case of absence. It is when knowledge is held by too few that problems occur. Don't forget to inform new staff of a pupil's medical needs and its consequences. This would include supply teachers, classroom workers and any lunchtime assistants.

In any medical emergency a teacher would be expected to take action. The essential point is that taking no action is more dangerous than assisting and getting it wrong. You can be reassured that legal action has never succeeded where medical assistance has been offered to pupils in good faith. So whilst a teacher can refuse to administer medicine, they must still be prepared to take emergency action. No teacher can walk away from a situation, because they would not be fulfilling their overriding duty of care.

You can turn to health professionals for specific advice on different conditions. For example the local consultant in communicable disease control will advise about infectious diseases. Support groups and voluntary organizations that specialize in particular conditions often produce support materials for schools. You also need to be aware of government guidelines as published on the Internet.

Allowing children to receive medication during the school day will help to minimize the amount of teaching missed. However, it is more sensible if it can be prescribed at intervals that enable it to be taken outside school hours and parents should be advised of this. This would resolve inevitable transportation and storage difficulties, as well as ease fears over identification. How is a member of staff to know what the child is taking? Is it really what it says on the tin? Requirements such as 'To be taken 30 minutes before food' can prove awkward and dis- ruptive to a class as a whole. You need to use your common sense in these situations.

Remember, teachers should not give non-prescribed medication to pupils. They are not in a position to know about any possible adverse reactions or whether a previous dose has been administered. The current guidelines from the DfES on aspirin are specific. It should never be given to a child under 16 unless prescribed by a doctor. You must always refuse those children who ask for painkillers. Phoning home for authorization isn't the answer either, since it brings with it difficulties over identification and accountability. If a pupil suffers regularly from acute pain, such as migraine or a difficult menstrual cycle, then the parents should be asked to supply appropriate painkillers, together with written instructions on their administration. Staff should then inform parents of the details of time, date and dose whenever it has been administered.

It is important that children are not denied access to education because of manageable medical requirements. Schools must accept that a pupil will need support if the effects of their condition on their progress are to be minimized. That support can only be provided if information is shared. Individual healthcare plans should be drawn up in partnership with parents, covering the administration of medicines and action to be taken in an emergency. It is an opportunity to clarify the support required, to identify any restrictions on participation and to determine levels of responsibility. Schools will need to take medical advice from health professionals. We can judge a child's educational needs but we are not in a position to make judgements about medication and treatment. It will also be an opportunity to raise any concerns about the school's ability to provide for particular needs.

This is clearly a worry and it is an area in which a healthcare plan would have particular importance. If a condition requires intimate or invasive treatment there is always an anxiety that this could lead to accusations of abuse. A particular example is the administration of diazepam. This can be prescribed to epileptic pupils in some circumstances and it may need to be administered rectally. The school should always try to ensure that where such treatment is necessary, two staff should be present, one of whom should be the same gender as the pupil. Efforts should be made to protect the dignity of the pupil at all times, even in an emergency.

A structured and well-documented approach, involving a health plan and accurate record-keeping is essential. Staff could be understandably reluctant to volunteer to carry out such treatment. If no member of staff is prepared to volunteer then the school should seek advice from the local Health Authority. Certainly don't feel obliged to volunteer yourself just because others won't. You have just as much right to refuse as anyone else. Schools must not hesitate to call emergency services if staff are unsure about what to do. Teachers are not expected to make judgements about health issues. Leave that to the professionals.

What you can do, however, is to set a positive example. Show the child and the rest of the school that you see the person behind the condition. It is surely a matter of principle that all pupils should be encouraged to take part in every aspect of school life. Your leadership should encourage integration and participation. It is what everyone deserves.

PART THREE

Dealing with
the wider world

33 Legal issues

Read widely and lead your staff

As time goes on I suspect that this will be the issue that dominates a deputy's working life. Yet it is the one about which I can write with the least confidence. There is constant change as the priorities within the law shift and strengthen. At the time of writing, there has been a focus upon the issue of consent. This implies the need for parents to be informed of any arrangements made for their children and the need to have written agreement that an activity will take place. Teachers have found themselves in difficulty where this has not happened. The willingness of parents to accept the professional judgement and direction of teachers has eroded in many cases. So teachers feel the need to be protected by the law. At the time of your reading this the emphasis might be very different, but I am sure that awareness of the law will feature highly amongst your priorities. You would be denying your responsibilities if you failed to keep yourself up-to-date with developments.

I have seen legal issues take increasing prominence in our daily work. All aspects of school life are now subject to legal interpretation – from admissions to pupil discipline to school visits to staffing issues. Schools have become a rich vein for the legal profession. It should be no surprise that there are specialists who now deal with legal issues in schools. And they will be coming your way. You need to be ready.

Take, for example, the *Freedom of Information Act 2005*. This placed upon schools a requirement to respond to enquiries from outside. Any information which a school holds must be provided on request. The public has a right to see hard copy, digital records and email communication. Any attempt to alter, delete or conceal information is a criminal offence. Your job first of all is to be aware of such requirements and then ensure that the staff are aware of what it all means. Ignorance is no defence. Suddenly you could be asked, 'How many bullying incidents did the school deal with last year?' Such a request could not be denied, but a well-informed school would also know that if such a request resulted in costs being incurred, then it would be legitimate to levy a charge for the time taken to collect such information.

The law can infiltrate all aspects of school life. Where do you stand if you are unhappy with the way a member of your staff dresses? The employment contract would imply that an employee should dress in a manner appropriate to work in a school. Any specific regulations the school might wish to put in place should be lawful and reasonable. This is all well and good. But a dress code extends beyond restrictions on clothing and covers issues such as hair styles, facial hair, make-up and piercings. When you start to deal with such issues you must try to be consistent and manage the sort of tensions that these issues can generate. A dispute can lead to all sorts of things – claims of unfair dismissal, gender discrimination, religious discrimination or of the breach of human rights. You cannot impose your own taste with regard to particular items of clothing, but T-shirts with offensive material could lead to dismissal. You can see just how quickly things can escalate.

What is your school's view of suntan lotion? Is it essential if students are exposed to the sun for an extended period whilst under the direction of the school? Are you going to insist that it is applied? And if you do, what about a child who might have an undisclosed skin allergy? And can your staff spray it on? And if so who rubs it in?

Much of what has happened reflects unreasonable fears by parents, a sense that things are falling apart and that the old certainties can no longer be trusted. Teachers who were once respected professionals in their community are now seen differently. They have always been fallible but now there is blame. And if to err is certainly human, to forgive is to deny yourself compensation. Whilst there is a belief that big money pay-outs are settled whenever Tania burns herself because she wasn't listening when her class was told how to use a glue gun, then the law will cast a long dark shadow over our working days. It is vital that the school has sufficient knowledge to be able to deal confidently with potentially damaging – and certainly time-wasting –

claims. You need to protect yourself. It is worthwhile subscribing to one of the specialist publications that will keep you up-to-date with changes and with the implications of decisions made in court. Conferences organized by legal experts and by professional associations are vital forums. You will pick up information from experts. You will develop your confidence. Someone from your school must attend at least one every year. What are your obligations to educate sick children? What are the implications of not storing student records efficiently? And what happens when things do go wrong? Who has liability? The employer? Or the individual employee? How else are you going to know the ways in which you are making yourself vulnerable if you don't listen to an expert?

Potentially difficult subjects are school trips and visits. You need to keep yourself fully informed about the complex implications when anything like this is organized because teachers can be extremely vulnerable. Pupils with medical needs should never be excluded from taking part in trips and visits, but staff involved need to be fully informed of any potential implications. At least one member of staff should be a competent first aider. Some trips might require personal support and, indeed, in some circumstances such as an overseas trip, it would be good practice to take the child's parent. This would enable staff to concentrate upon the health and safety of the party as a whole.

A parent and child may belong to a religious body that repudiates certain medical treatments. This poses particular complications where school trips are involved. In an emergency, a teacher who could not obtain specific parental instructions would need to employ standard medical treatment, in order to discharge their own duty of care. If a child is on a trip and the parent is not prepared to give written instructions on the subject of medical treatment, then the pupil should not join the party. You might like to reflect at this point about how something that was once so simple now definitely is no such thing. All I can say is that you must never overlook the legal implications of the things that schools and teachers do.

The use of computers in school has a legal dimension and is an example of how the law has had to re-position itself to respond to the ways that society changes. The school, for example, is entitled to limit its employees' use of its IT systems, including email and the Internet. Viewing certain sites could, for example, be regarded as gross misconduct and lead to dismissal. Such regulations were obviously not required only a few years ago. Now a whole new and unmapped minefield exists. If a member of staff is using email at work to send or receive inappropriate comments or material, then there is the possibility for messages sent from the school to have a negative impact on the school's reputation. And the potential for disaster is huge. A comment about a difficult child, or sensitive information about a family, could so easily end up on the wrong computer, either through a simple mistake or by being forwarded. So it is essential that staff are aware of what represents acceptable email use. Basically, if you are not comfortable with the possibility of the message's content becoming public then you probably shouldn't send it. Internet and email policies are fast becoming a provision of most employment contracts.

Not only do you have an obligation to keep yourself up-to-date, but also you must ensure that your staff, both teaching and non-teaching, are kept aware of the implications of what they do. Requirements and advice about school visits is an important example. They are likely to involve quite a number of staff over the years and they must therefore be aware of the consequences and vulnerabilities that attach themselves when things go wrong. It is a good idea to set aside time in a staff meeting to look at the law. You can do this by using case studies. 'This is what happened when . . .' This can be both entertaining and informative. Remember, one of your responsibilities is to become informed in these matters, one who can lead the staff and add to their professional awareness.

Naturally, if things go badly wrong with a member of staff and disciplinary procedures lead to dismissal, you will need to have access to the very best advice. It would be inappropriate to comment on specifics here for they will vary, but you must ensure that all procedures are followed precisely and that everything is carefully documented. It is through a variance from established and agreed processes that you are in danger of losing any appeal.

This section can go on and on. There are books to be written on individual aspects of the law in schools that will be much longer than this one. All I can do is to encourage you to keep up-to-date. Any investment you make in your own knowledge and in the training of your staff will never be wasted.

34 Work–life balance

Too much work is likely to make you unbalanced

It is your job as deputy to manage the school. Obviously you will also be offering leadership and vision, but ultimately it is your job to make sure that all runs smoothly every day. In the end, if you are going to make things happen then that requires you to manage people. Remember: systems, details and projects all change. One thing, however, remains constant: teachers will complain.

There is nothing else known to man that can provoke the instinctive need of teachers to complain as much as the issue of workload. They will attempt to outdo each other with stories of pain and sorrow. Underpaid, undervalued, overlooked. Treated as mushrooms (you know the story, kept in the dark and occasionally pelted with manure). Lions led by donkeys. If you haven't heard this then you haven't been in a staffroom recently. You know the place – that repository of suffering.

The leadership team of course doesn't care and merely keeps on piling on to them pointless tasks designed to destroy their sense of well-being and psychic balance. They don't know what they are doing, they don't know what it is like, they haven't got the marking, they haven't got the contact time, they haven't got a clue. Teaching, the perfect job? Don't make me laugh. It is certainly true that the professionalism of teachers and their dedication to the institution in which they work has been exploited in the past to get jobs done on the cheap. But the job is never going to be the sort of job that ends at 3.30pm. That is the reason that we get the holidays. As compensation for all those long evenings correcting the illegible and assessing the illogical.

Don't be too downhearted if your exciting new idea is greeted with groans and depression. Don't take it personally. Everyone, whatever it is that they do, complains about their job. The girls who attended the Greek gods, playing ethereal tunes on the harp and scattering rose petals before them, were really hacked off by that clinging smell. No, it is human nature to complain about work. In order to work you sacrifice your freedom in exchange for money. But everyone has days when that deal doesn't seem a fair one. What you must do as deputy is to separate out the genuine and justifiable complaints from the unstructured background noise that thrives in every workplace.

Teaching is a demanding job. That is never going to change. Those demands and their satisfactions should be what brought us into the job in the first place. It is unreasonable of some staff to expect anything different. Stress and pressure are quite normal things. It is when the structures that you are responsible for putting into place turn these things into unmanageable monsters causing unnecessary distress that you must act. Everyone has a right to expect a rich and satisfying quality of life and work mustn't stop that happening. But in many ways work–life balance is something that you need to manage for yourself. You can try to legislate in order to help others achieve it but they need to manage it themselves. That is where the problems arise.

Take parent consultation evenings as an example. You can take the decision to make them shorter. You are thus showing a desire to help staff. But it is then up to them to manage these shorter evenings. They are the ones who have to talk less. If they play the martyr in an attempt to be the last to leave, then who was it who made that decision? Here's a clue. It wasn't you. Certainly by reducing the workload you won't automatically bring about a better balance between school and home. Your staff have got to want this and show a willingness to take the opportunities. Of course, there are things that you can do. You can cut down on the number of meetings. Always ask yourself if a meeting is really necessary. Is there a worthwhile agenda? Is it going to be productive? Can it be moved to a better time? You can also think about trying to even out the peaks and troughs of a teacher's workload by shifting things like exams and reports to different times of the year. Look carefully at the school calendar and use your experience to identify the likely pressure points. Perhaps most importantly you need to talk to your staff in an open and honest way. Tell them that they should be more disciplined on consultation evenings. Tell them that you want all staff cars out of the car park by 4.00pm on Friday. Make work–life balance an issue and your colleagues may then find it easier to follow a path towards it.

It is a sad life and an unfulfilled one if there are things you want to do and you can do them, but you don't because work gets in the way.

That is how I came to writing. I wanted to do it. I have always worked hard at my job in whichever school I have been working, but having spent all my time in the classroom commenting on the writing of others, I always wanted to discover whether I could do it for myself. And no one was going to find the time for me to find that out. The only person who could find the time for me to try it out was myself. And that is what everyone must do. Make the time for the things that are important. No one will ever congratulate you on the scope of your unfulfilled dreams. And you have to work this out for yourself. Whilst you must try your best to ensure that the school doesn't prevent the rest of the staff achieving such a balance, no one makes the same efforts on your behalf. You must deal with these things yourself.

It is a hard thing to deal with but ask yourself what your school wants from you. It wants clarity of leadership and inspiration. How are those things to be achieved? By constantly running around the school fire-fighting student behaviour? Or through the sort of reflection that comes from a healthy and focused mind? The school will not get the best out of you by allowing you to be driven into the ground. The only person who can stop this happening isn't the head, it is you. This means that you shouldn't feel guilty if you sometimes put yourself first. You may feel that it is your obligation to put the rest of the staff first, rather like the impoverished mother who feeds her children from her own mouth. And as deputy you will deal with other people's needs before you deal with your own. But just occasionally you have to take your own work–life balance in hand. You don't have to be the last person to leave in the building in the evening. You have as much right as anyone to accompany your partner or child to a medical appointment. Don't marginalize your own needs to the extent that they are completely ignored. It is not always simple to achieve. Perhaps what the phrase work–life balance means is that you need to work hard to achieve a life balance. But you must do it for yourself or you will turn around and it will be too late. Unless you take control of this, then school will consume every part of you.

35 Emergencies

Your responsibility is to lead the community

You will have become a deputy head as a result of your excellence in the arena of education, your area of expertise. But now you will need to become familiar with a wider world. You will need to be familiar with legislation and regulations and prepare your school to handle small problems and big disasters. Few will forgive you if you handle a situation inappropriately through lack of preparation. You are there to handle emergencies on behalf of the school and the people who work and learn there. There are all sorts of emergencies. The science teacher's kitchen ceiling falls in and it certainly is a domestic emergency. The school will want to support as best it can because this is what holds workforces together. But this is not an emergency for the school. It is a question of cover, leave of absence, help.

The real emergencies you might have to deal with as a school run much deeper. You will hope that you'll never have to deal with one. Aggressive parents will come your way. But violent ones? Let's hope not. A child breaks a leg on a skiing trip. Very possible. But something worse? It probably won't happen. But it might, and there are courses available that will prepare you for such a disaster. It is important that someone on the leadership team has some awareness of how to react. Your own responses in an emergency might not easily be predicted, but you do need a framework within which to place them. Of course, huge regional and national emergencies are not your responsibility. You don't have to work out a strategy. But you do need to know where you fit into the overall scheme of things. You must be familiar with the necessary government websites that carry the latest information in a variety of scenarios. Try www.teachernet.gov.uk/emergencies. It is something that you need to check at least once a term. It is all part of keeping informed. As you will see when you examine the underlying principles, whilst you can't always prepare for the specifics of a problem, you can raise your own awareness and that of the governing body.

In the first place, you need to find out about the Local Authority's Critical Incident or Civil Contingency plans. It might be that your school has already been designated as an emergency shelter if there was need for an evacuation in your area. In any emergency you will need to know what your role is. Your prime responsibility must be for people, not property, and most importantly for your students. You will know them, they will know you and they will trust you. In any difficult situation they will automatically look to you for leadership. That is what you should deal with in the first instance, the students and the staff who know you. Don't worry about anything else. If it is possible then you should be able to pass over media handling to others, though obviously much depends upon the nature of the incident.

Like all places of employment, a school must keep statutory accident records and your school needs to be aware of current regulations. You will need to be aware of the Reporting of Injuries, Diseases and Dangerous Occurrences Regulations 1995 (RIDDOR) which require some accidents to be reported to the Health and Safety Executive. These would generally involve accidents resulting in death or major injury. Of course regulations change, but you need to know where to go to check whether they have. That place is probably your LEA or a government website. There is certainly no good reason why you shouldn't be properly informed.

In the case of fire, again there are regulations that require all workplaces to have an emergency plan. Your evacuation procedures should be well-rehearsed and there should be a drill once a term. Don't forget that new students and visitors to the school will need to be aware of what they should do. Close contact with local fire officers is especially important. They will wish to be involved in schools anyway as a preventative measure. In circumstances where you have false and malicious alarms, they are always ready to speak to perpetrators. They are keen to minimize risks and to protect means of escape. Of course, procedures and systems should already be well established in your school. The DfES has Guidance on Fire Safety which your school should know about. It may not be your responsibility to know these details but it is your responsibility to ensure that the responsible person does.

Fire is dangerous. So is water. The consequences of a flood can be as equally devastating as a fire. Any school in an area prone to flooding should have a plan. You will need to know where flood water can enter and you will need to ensure that the school stores vulnerable and dangerous materials in high places, away from the possibility of water contamination. The government has set procedures that can be implemented if there is sufficient warning, but no one should be asked to do things that are beyond their competence to carry them out. These tasks might involve disconnecting appliances or services. Afterwards, contamination issues will have to be addressed. It is a dangerous time when diseases can spread and when dangerous objects like broken glass could be hidden, ready to slash the unwary. Once again, your job is to know where to get the information to minimize danger through raised awareness. It is not your job to pull on a big pair of rubber boots and unblock the drains.

Major security issues are not things that you can prepare for specifically. This book is not intended to give advice on terrorism or terrorist activity. You need to maintain a close relationship with the police and involve them the minute you have a concern. But it should be clear to you what your professional duty should be. As a deputy head your first concern must be the safety of students. That must come before anything else. It is to act in this way that you have been granted seniority and you must fulfil that expectation.

36 Dealing with parents

Don't kid yourself. A difficult parent is on their way to see you soon

An emergency that is quite likely to occur is the appearance on school premises of an unhappy or aggressive adult. No matter is so small that a bored or unhappy member of the community will not regard it as an opportunity to rush up to the school for a confrontation.

Dealing with parents is a high-risk issue. The potential for violence that it brings is considered by some to be one of the most serious problems that teachers face. Your position as a senior manager in the school can put you right in the front line. Anyone dealing directly with the public can face aggressive or violent behaviour and schools are no different.

There is considerable anecdotal evidence that parents are becoming more troublesome and more willing to take issue with teachers. The reasons for this are many and varied, but it is clear that as the status of teachers has declined, so the public are less inclined to treat the profession with respect. Further, schools are accessible, at the heart of the communities that they serve. That is how we want them to be. But some of those communities are fractured and if you haven't got a job or much to do, then no matter is too small to warrant a little trip up to school to have a word with teacher. You don't have to get on a bus. It is close enough for you to be still steamed up when you get there, just a little stroll along the road. If you do not have positive memories of school yourself, you might still regard education as neither a force for change nor for good but rather as an imposition from an official world, one you might feel has never treated you particularly well. Teachers are your daily contact with that world.

You might think it would be better if we kept everyone out of our buildings. We can't. On the one hand we say we want to be open and welcoming places for everyone. On the other hand, teachers and pupils must be allowed to work and learn in a safe and secure environment. But the shadow of Dunblane hangs over us all. So, until we ring-fence our schools with barbed wire and turn them into fortresses, we will have to manage a complex situation – and stay measured. After all, to conduct learning in an atmosphere of siege and apprehension is not ideal. Schools were never intended to be secure institutions. They are part of their communities and they serve different purposes to different people. Certainly, as the emphasis on Community Education grows, more and more people are coming into secondary schools. As a result, it is becoming very hard for you to know who all the adults are on school premises at any one time.

The design of schools too militates against security. Often we work on large and untidy sites with long perimeters. Sometimes there are separate buildings commanding majestic views of the playing fields which themselves can blur the boundaries of the school. Of course, the bigger the school the more exits that are required for safety reasons. And every exit can become an entrance, through carelessness or design. One of the problems is that parents often think that schools are public places. Because their children go there every day and have a free run of the place they think they should too. But this is not the case.

Schools are not public places to which anyone can have access. Anyone who enters without permission is a trespasser and you can ask them to leave. If you, or a member of staff, feels they are under threat then that is the least you can do. No one has an unrestricted right of access and parents should act as any other visitors to school. But they might need help to make sure they do. This means that there should be clear signs indicating where visitors should present themselves. You will never inhibit a determined intruder but you will be avoiding any ambiguity and you will be able to invite anyone to leave who will not follow your guidelines.

There should be an overall policy for security in all schools based upon their own circumstances. It is vital that the leadership team is seen to implement the policy and to show that they are actively committed to the safety of staff and pupils. There must be a declaration of unwavering support for any colleague who has been assaulted or has suffered verbal abuse. There should be a promise that all incidents will be investigated and that all will be reported to the police. There should be standard letters that can be issued to those who make threats or verbally abuse any employees. You should never hesitate in sending them out. Obviously, good record keeping will help to identify patterns of behaviour and should be available to be passed on responsibly on pupil transfer. If Krystle in Year 7 has a dodgy father, then the primary partner school should have told you about this. All new staff must be aware of the policy, for they could be at greater risk if they don't know what to do in challenging circumstances.

A fundamental priority must be access control. Any visitors to the school should know exactly where they should go and what they should do from prominently displayed information. Schools always have visitors – book reps, delivery men, those who unblock the drains, parents – and they should all be treated in the same way. They should follow the clear signs to the reception area where they should be signed in and authorized. A well-managed and welcoming reception area should offer a helpful service rather than overt security measures. In larger schools it might be necessary to establish which is the main entrance that visitors should use. Of course this can put the office staff in the front line for dealing with troubled visitors so it is important that they are not isolated. Don't forget that they are especially vulnerable to unwelcome visitors. You need to make sure that they have the necessary training and any structures and equipment that can offer them reassurance. The ability to close a door on someone who makes them uncomfortable is always an advantage. You will work as a team in the school and there is nowhere more important than in the administrative area where those with a grudge are likely to turn up. If everyone watches out for each other the feeling of security will increase. No one should have any hesitation about dialling 999 if matters seem to be particularly unpleasant. It is always better to be safe. It is always a help if you can encourage parents to make an appointment to see someone, if only to ensure that they are indeed available. This can be an important way of reducing frustrations and anger and also for preparing yourself for such an interview.

Everyone has a right to complain and most of us have done so at sometime or other. As customers we have expectations and rights so as teachers we can hardly expect to be treated any differently. If a parent is unhappy then they have every right to complain, just as we have ourselves. It is the manner in which it is done that is important. If customers have a complaint then perhaps the knowledge that they can see the manager, who will give them time and listen to what they have to say, will offer reassurance. If it works in shops then it ought to work in schools. If the leadership team is accessible and sympathetic then a great many problems can be solved at an early stage. Often just a sight of someone in a suit is all that is needed.

However, there will come a point at which firm words will be needed and you mustn't shy away from this moment if it is your judgement that this is required. You can't be unfailingly polite to people who wander in off the street and shout abuse, especially at staff who are in the front line. There is no excuse for bad manners and there is no reason why you should go on giving people time and a space if they continue to be unreasonable. If they want to shout about the bus service then that's fine, but no one should unload on those who have nothing to do with such a problem. There comes a point where you have to say no. It is just that it is difficult to judge when that point has been reached.

You will need to establish a complaints procedure if you haven't already got one and people need to know about it. They need to know how to proceed and to whom they should go. Never assume that all the parents in your community know how to do it. Indeed, any aggression may in part reflect a lack of confidence in their own ability to deal with difficult situations. As the professional it is your job to offer guidance and support. Listen to what they have to say and help them structure their complaint. It is in this way that you will develop a reputation as a confident and approachable school, which will create the sort of climate in which difficulties can be resolved.

I suppose we need to ask ourselves who are these people who are complaining. The answer must be that they are us. A difficult parent is perhaps just a caring one. Perhaps we all have the capacity to be difficult if we are sufficiently provoked. This is something we mustn't forget. We are all programmed to support our children. Why shouldn't we stand up for them if we feel that they have been badly treated? Of course, it is the manner in which this is done that provokes bigger issues. In socially disadvantaged areas, the parents are not always aware of how to pursue a complaint formally. They may be moved to anger far more quickly because they feel threatened or insulted.

The trigger may have been something as simple as an intrusive assignment that seems to probe too deeply into family affairs, but the cause is, generally, something physical. Perhaps a bullying incident remains unsatisfactorily resolved, perhaps it's the overspill from a playground argument. Or perhaps, as sometimes happens, the child has not told the complete truth about an incident.

If a parent bypasses the main administrative area of the school and appears in a classroom then there has already been a security failure. You have an intruder. Since they have not gone through your clearly defined system then you can only assume that their purpose is questionable. Statistically, an intruder will generally be an ex-student or a parent who will know where they are going and who they want to see. So you must also assume that they are unhappy. Not only is it unlikely that they are going to heap praise upon the French teacher, but also you can never be sure if the mood of your visitor has been chemically enhanced. At this point you have to rely upon the professionalism of your staff and hope that they manage to defuse the situation. It is a good idea if someone has already spoken to staff, perhaps in a training session, about what they should do in this circumstance. When you turn up what you must try to do is to guide the intruder away from the classroom and away to your office. Ensure, if you can, that others around know that you are dealing with an incident and let them contact the police if they feel it is appropriate. You must remain calm. It is easier said than done, but your priority must be to defuse the situation. So avoid looking aggressive. Don't put your hands on your hips, don't wag any fingers, don't become officious. Speak slowly so that you are not drawn into a heated argument. But take the initiative. In these circumstances your job is to stand between the adult and your member of staff, both literally and metaphorically. These situations are ones in which many teachers feel vulnerable. It would not be unusual for them to have caused a problem but to be unable to deal with the consequences when it backfires. It up to you to take ownership. You need to shepherd any intruder towards your office and away from a public arena where events can escalate very quickly. It is easier to deal with this sort of visitor in a controlled environment of your own choosing.

How you behave yourself is very important. You have the position of authority and others will feel they are talking to a decision maker when they come to you. This is probably what they wanted. They will want to make a complaint about something, or more usually someone.

They will believe you are in a position to do something about it. Listen carefully to what they have to say and in the first few moments maintain eye contact. Then, when the initial statement has been made, let them see that you are making some notes. It always makes visitors feel important that you are recording what they say. Documents mean that you are taking them seriously. Keep them talking as long as you can. Whilst they are talking they are not hitting. Once the crisis has been negotiated, then your responsibility is to prevent the possibility of a repeat performance. Send out your official letters, but also make sure that you stick to your word. What did you say? You will look into their complaint, you will speak to someone, you will keep in touch. If you said you were going to set up a meeting or telephone at a specific time then do so. The fact that they didn't deal with their complaint properly doesn't negate the nature of their original complaint. They might still have a valid point to make. So you must still be ready to look into it. In this way, you will establish your reputation as someone who keeps their word and thus the chances of a repeat will be reduced. But don't feel inhibited about making the fundamental point that whatever their grievance, their action in avoiding established procedures was wrong and must not be repeated.

You might want to examine the way in which technology can help to offer security to your staff but you mustn't get seduced by it. Most technology, like video surveillance, offers some reassurance but does little to prevent incidents happening. Further, a panic alarm, audible or otherwise, has the capacity to change a minor incident into a major one. What happens when it goes off? Who responds and how quickly can they do it? Remember, if an assault is to happen, it happens in seconds, not minutes. And what happens if no one responds? This will suggest that there is no one around at all. The most effective way of dealing with intruders is together, as a collective. Mutual support is the most important element of all.

Staff need to approach unidentified visitors and ask them if they can help. You also need to involve the pupils in this too, asking them to report any suspicious behaviour immediately. Usually they are very good and very sensible where this is concerned. The way the leadership team is perceived is a crucial element in all this. If parents feel valued and listened to, respected as part of a partnership, then they will happily follow the proper procedures because they know they will be taken seriously. They must know that if they have a problem then you will help them to resolve it. You must never be too proud to say that you have got something wrong. It is about reputation and commitment and expectations.

Never forget that the vast majority of parents are sensible and supportive. They may well question some of the things that we do and during our careers we are bound to meet parents who are unhappy with our performance, but that is all part of a mature relationship. Parents have a right to expect the very best for their child and they also have a right to express their concerns. As a profession we should welcome such dialogue. We cannot always expect it on our terms. We are not under siege, we are not victims. We need to be confident and approachable for the good of our students and for the communities where we work. There are nutters out there but they should not be allowed to set the agenda. Don't forget, if our job is about anything at all it is about managing people, big and small. We are good at it.

37 The press

Stay calm. Journalists aren't stupid

An experienced headteacher once told me, 'If you live by the press, sooner or later you will die by the press. Don't get involved.' Life in schools these days is not so simple. Whilst you shouldn't court attention, it doesn't mean that you should lock yourself away from the glare of publicity. Moderation in all things. And anyway, no school can exist outside of the area where it is located. That location is often defined by its newspaper. Remember, Jason's dad, unhappy at your decision to send him home, might try to drop the school in it by contacting the local press. Parents often use this as a threat. Of course, they are in no position to know whether the paper will be at all interested in the colour of Jason's hair, but there are such things as slow news days. Nonetheless, you cannot possibly show that you are in anyway intimidated by such threats. In these circumstances I always find it helps to offer an angry parent the phone number of the local paper. It suggests confidence and gives an impression of balance and control. Don't forget, the press will be equally aware that some parents are strange and will not want to make themselves look foolish by running some half-baked nonsense on page 3. They will always phone up to check the details of any story they have been offered. So remain calm and adopt the sort of air that suggests you can't understand why anyone is worrying so much about something so trivial.

You can manage such a situation more confidently if you have established a relationship with the local press. Always be prepared to speak to the editor and reporters. Give them helpful quotes and comments when they ask for them on generic educational issues and always be ready to promote the successes of the school and to defend its decisions. Which naturally presupposes that you are not going to make stupid indefensible ones. This is, of course, very hard to guarantee. If someone has messed up then tell the press that you will consult and review and meet. Don't add any further idiocy as the icing on top of a moment of stupidity. If it is all going pear-shaped, then take advice from the LEA if you can, who will probably speak on your behalf, or consult your professional association. But also remember that the vast majority of issues disappear just as quickly as they emerge. Today it may be news; tomorrow it is likely to have been blown around a lamp post.

If you can anticipate an issue is going to provoke interest, then it is a good idea to plan out what you are going to say beforehand. Write it down. In a moment of crisis it is a good idea to give someone the responsibility for dealing with the media. Make sure that there is a press statement ready. But remember that the press are not always on your side. They want their story and *they* will establish the angle they are to pursue. You cannot control this. However professional you believe you are, others will want a story with a different emphasis. No matter how clever you think you are, they can run rings around you, then chew you up and spit you out. That is when you need that relationship.

Journalists are always looking for good news stories and photographs of students. They can sometimes have space they need to fill and things like this sell papers. They can phone up and ask for something for page 7 and on occasions like this it is useful to know exactly what's going on in your school. Sports and drama achievements, environmental and community work. If you don't have this information then pass them on to someone who does. An appearance in the newspaper in this way can be valuable publicity. They will want names and often the particular part of your catchment area where a student lives. They know their job. They know what sells. And if you have worked with them before in this way, then it makes it easier to deal with the local deviant complaining about Year 10 sitting on a wall outside the chip shop. The first thing they will do is to phone you.

If you do think that the school is going to feature in the press, then make sure that the head knows. If they are out at a meeting they do not want to be cornered unexpectedly by a local councillor or governor asking tricky questions about something they know nothing about.

Inform the chair of governors and if necessary contact the LEA. They will have people there who are ready to deal with reporters.

Just as there are good and bad teachers, so there are also good and bad reporters. When you get slime balls outside the school gate questioning students about rumours they've picked up – usually sexually orientated ones are the greatest attraction – you can inform the police. Don't hesitate. They are not there to help either you or your community. Schools are naturally full of children and thus are a focus for sensitive concerns. Those concerns become urgent in many eyes when safety and protection are involved. A scary story that suggests children are at risk sells papers. And sex sells papers best of all. When the sharks are circling in this way, then there are some difficult decisions to be made. It is obvious that you need to think about what you are saying but you must also cooperate as much as you feel able to do. The judgement is that they are going to write something anyway, so it might be best to have some involvement in it. Once you appear to have something to hide, then you can easily be misrepresented. That is when it becomes really difficult. But the essential truth is that you have a right to choose who to speak to and when.

The media exists in so many forms – newspapers, television, radio, both local and national – that a big story exposes many different tentacles of the octopus that is trying to ensnare you. If you think this might happen then consider going ex-directory, for they will have no hesitation in tracking you down at home. You have a right to expect privacy, whatever has occurred.

Whatever has happened, whether bereavement or accident or scandal, and no matter how much you might get caught up in media management and press statements and interviews, remember that your first job is to keep the school calm. You need to protect the students and you need to ensure that you fulfil your primary objective, which is to educate them without distractions or dramas.

But, of course, not all your dealings with the press will be negative ones. Student achievements, the winning of awards, special events, they are all things that the community want to hear about and to celebrate. These are legitimate interests and you must be ready to oblige because it is what your community wants. And if you do these things, then it makes the other stuff easier to handle.

38 How your school is judged

Invest in your students. They are the ones who define your school for others

In the end, your school is judged on the basis of its students. The local community has little knowledge or understanding of your all-encompassing vision for staff training or for equal opportunities. Their impressions of the school could well be based upon how six members of Year 10 behave outside the sweet shop at lunchtime. Of course, we like to believe that the way we are perceived is on the basis of our professional standards, our examination success, our league-table position, our Investors in People status. But the reputation of the school rests upon its students and the things some of them do that are wrong. When the girls in Year 8 kick up the bulbs in the park it is news. When the boys in Year 9 help an old lady with her laundry it isn't. It is a fact of life. So you are always polite to complainants, you always look into their problem, you always call them back. This is all part of the picture that forms about the school and once formed it takes ages to restore.

You must try to influence the students by passing on worthwhile values and a sense of responsibility, but always be aware that your school could easily be condemned for things over which you have little influence. As a result you become reactive. You respond to bad behaviour on the buses and deal with the issue. But there is little you could have done to have prevented it. Just be seen to deal with it in a serious and meaningful way. Never dismiss a complaint out of hand because you never know what the consequences might be.

Important people who make judgements on the school are the governors. They are very important, connecting the school with its own community and ensuring there is a level of accountability. Where a selective secondary system exists then that accountability is reduced, because the community that is served by the school is fragmented. Not everyone who attends the school lives where it is situated and if places in it are hard to win, then there is going to be less willingness to question what happens. But in other schools which serve a defined catchment area, well-known governors are often the first to be approached when a problem arises. This can mean that governors make schools more responsive, more likely to sustain community support, because they are a symbol of who the school belongs to. They are there to govern, not to manage, so they must trust their leadership team to manage the school on behalf of the community. But there is nothing wrong with them asking the leadership team to justify what they have decided and what they have done. In this way the reputation of the school will be enhanced.

The other way in which judgements are made about the school is through the inspection process. The point about inspections is that no matter how stressful teachers might find them, society has the right to find out what is happening in its schools. Schools must be accountable and mustn't be frightened of that accountability. It is a legitimate requirement of schools to accommodate and then act upon the judgements of others. Of course, teachers find them difficult but that is no reason to stop them happening. You cannot elevate a teacher's wishes above the right of a society to know how schools are performing. You need to keep this firmly in your mind and in the minds of your colleagues. Apart from anything else, if you have all been doing your job properly you should approach an inspection with confidence and welcome the confirmation of your success that it brings. Of course, this is hardly the occasion to introduce any changes or new initiatives. Why should you? Everything is fine and under control. Apart from anything else, when the envelope with the invitation that you just can't refuse arrives, it is too late to make any effective changes anyway.

When it is inspection time, your duty is naturally to lead the school and the staff through this stressful period. It is obvious isn't it? You are not allowed to show any of the symptoms of pre-inspection disorder. You must remain calm and confident, dismissive of the intrusion. Through you, the school will advertise the fact that it has nothing to fear. You will want the school to be seen in the best possible light because, of course, everything is just dandy. The school needs merely to run normally. Which is fine, because you will spend most of your time managing staff emotions. Initially they will be anxious and tense. This is natural and not necessarily a bad thing. You will offer reassurance and support. After all, you know already what is going on in your school. As you will say to your staff, 'I can write that report for them now.' And so you should. It is your school.

Never forget that an inspection involves the whole school. It is not something dreamed up to punish teachers alone. Your support staff and your administrative colleagues will probably have very strong feelings for the school and will want it to succeed. They certainly won't want to feel that they have let the school down in some way. If things do go wrong they can take it personally — especially those involved in classroom support. They will carry a sense of responsibility and you must show them that they are valued but never culpable. They are not teachers after all.

Office staff need to be reassured that the inspectors are not the enemy, trained to catch them out. They are there to help the school do its job better. So they must not worry about any conversations they might have with the inspection team. They must be as open and as honest as they always are. They may be parents of students in the school themselves, so they have a vested interest in making it a better place.

In the end, just as the community makes its judgements, so does the inspection team. Any judgements made about the school are made on the basis of the students themselves. How well do they learn? How well do they achieve? What sort of effect does the teaching have? Whatever ways are determined for finding the answers to these things, they must involve some element of classroom observation. For most teachers this is quite difficult, even though lesson observation has become an everyday part of the modern school experience. To be observed by your colleagues who share the same daily experience as yourself is one thing, but to be watched by a humourless stranger with a clipboard is quite another. It is neither inspiring nor uplifting. But as the deputy you must be different. However you feel yourself, you must be seen to be inviting strangers to watch your lessons. Of course, most teachers find this difficult. But of course you don't. You are a leader and so you are confident and relaxed. Always give time to your colleagues during the time of the inspection. They might need reassurance or help, they might want to talk. Give them that time. Help from you, commiserations, a pat on the back, mean a lot, because of your status in the school. Never forget that.

The important thing about inspections is that really they should only ever confirm what you know about the school already. Any judgement which indicates that there are serious weaknesses in an area of the school is, in the end, a judgement on the leadership team of which you are a part. If the inspection contradicts what you think, then you haven't been doing your job properly. And if you knew something was dodgy, what strategies did you put in place to rectify this? And if you didn't know, then what have you been doing? Not to know about the strengths and weaknesses of your own school implies that the leadership team is failing. This is why it is important that when you know something, you have responded with an action plan and that you have monitored it. You can't rely upon the inspection team to put things right. They don't exist to do your dirty work for you. They can't. They arrive, they see, they go. You stay and you are the one who has to lead the underperforming areas out of the darkness and into the bright light of achievement and fulfilment. That is what your job is about.

PART FOUR

Moving on

39 Moving on

Your motivation comes from within

The job of deputy head has to be seen as an end in itself. It can never be merely a stepping stone to something else. If that something else never comes, then the deputy will be dithering in no man's land and their commitment will wither. And in this job commitment is everything.

It is true that the adverts frequently say that successful candidates for a deputy head post will be keen to move on to headship. Why is this regarded as being so important? It speaks of vision and purpose. They want someone who will take on the challenge, who will have a reason to innovate and to seek improvement, not someone who will be happy to slip into comfortable insignificance. But promotion isn't the only reason why you need to show such qualities. You should have a need within yourself to do things properly. The governors have displayed their faith in you by giving you the job. You need to repay that faith by leading the community in a bright and vibrant fashion. If promotion comes, then you should celebrate the way in which the opportunities you have had have prepared you for it. The school has played a part in preparing you for this move. If it doesn't happen, and there may be many reasons why it doesn't, then you must still test yourself in school and drive things on because that is what you are paid to do. That is the obligation you accepted when you took the job on. And what the school expected when they took you on. You agreed to serve the school, not merely yourself.

You may wish actively to seek promotion and this, in itself, could have positive effects for the school. It would certainly be preferable to you simply waiting for your headteacher to announce his retirement due to a dicky heart, before you decide that you quite fancy the challenge of being a head and so might as well get an application form from the office. But this does not speak of drive and vision.

Always be clear about your skills and always be aware that one of your primary functions is to be ready to deputize for the headteacher. You need to be ready for that. You may not seek headship but it could be thrust upon you. The school needs you to be ready. So you will prepare yourself by honing your knowledge and skills.

If you decide to make an application you will need to pull all your ideas and plans into a coherent shape which could have particular benefits for your current school. It will make you think about what you are doing, it will spark off new ideas. The National Professional Qualification for Headship (NPQH) is now mandatory and the course will provide excellent professional development opportunities and first-rate networking. It will inevitably have an impact on the way you do your job. You will need to decide early in your appointment whether or not you intend to pursue the qualification. It is an important decision and you will need to think ahead. Without it you have no chance of making a shortlist. You might find some of the subject matter a little insulting, particularly if you have been a deputy for some time, since the course will deal with the everyday stuff of your working life as part of a modern leadership team. This should not, however, devalue the experience, for it should help anyone come to terms with the demands of their first headship, especially for an otherwise happy and convivial individual who might need to adjust to learning to live with the essential loneliness of their new job.

The course will bring professional benefits. It will be a forum in which you will meet other school leaders and find out more about what is going on elsewhere. You might be required to carry out a research project which will definitely give you an opportunity to reflect on your practice and your principles. If this does nothing else it will benefit your own school as well as possibly enhancing your own career. It is a payback to the school which has supported you in this application and helped to put you in a position where you can exploit the opportunities it presents. It could be something about the strategic use of IT or about raising standards of literacy and numeracy. You will have to read all those things that you have been meaning to read for some time and never ever found the time to do so. It is also a good opportunity to discover whether you really do want the Head's job. Now you know a little more, perhaps it isn't for you. Or perhaps you can't wait to get stuck in. In the end, it is probably better to do the course whether you are convinced about it or otherwise. By achieving the qualification, you are keeping your options open. However it turns out, it will not have wasted your time.

The big decision is, of course, how much you really want the job. Do you want the job so badly that you are prepared to move to the other side of the country? Or are you unwilling to uproot your family? If it is the former then you will almost certainly achieve your goal, unless you are in fact mind-numbingly incompetent. Of course, you may thus end up in one of the more unappealing parts of the country, but you have shown that this is a price that you are ready to pay. If your family is settled, or if you have unavoidable family obligations, then you may have to wait longer for an opportunity to arise, and with no guarantee of success. You are a grown-up person now. You must make your choice and be prepared to live with the consequences. That is why you must not rely upon promotion to provide you with motivation. It must ultimately come from within.

If you are determined to pursue a headship post, then as you trawl through the details of the schools from which you have requested information, you will pick up valuable hints and tips that can inform what you bring to your existing position and, as well, will filter into your next application. This will similarly be the case if and when you are called for interview. For anyone an interview is a stressful occasion, a time when you are expected to perform before an unfamiliar audience for an intense and extended period, an audience that has every right to scrutinize your every move. But you will learn things from this experience, about yourself and about your job that could be of benefit. That is the point. Everything that we are doing is a learning experience. We work in education, we believe in education, we must take from every experience ideas that will help us grow as people and help us do our job better.

For this reason, you should not regard any application you make as an act of betrayal. As long as you have been in your school for a reasonable length of time – and only you yourself will know how long that is – and you have made a memorable contribution to the whole of the school community, then you should make your application with confidence, not guilt. It may be that you will feel it necessary to review your position if you are making lots of interviews but are unsuccessful. Something isn't right and you are putting yourself through a great deal of unproductive turmoil and probably causing a great deal of disruption to your own school through your repeated absence. In addition, you might be harming your own reputation. Not only will you be seen as a careerist with no sense of balance or discrimination but also, more importantly, as an unsuccessful one. Why won't anyone else have you? You can be unlucky on a couple of occasions but repeated failure might make life very difficult for you. In such circumstances, perhaps you might need to reassess your priorities, before your colleagues decide to reassess your reputation. Remember the need for balance in all things.

40 A career plan?

At the cost of your happiness?

There is a truth that looks down upon us all. We can all get promoted. And we can all keep on being promoted if we try hard enough, if we devote our lives to our careers. Until one day we are appointed to a job that we cannot do. Each step up the ladder is based upon our previous or current success. None of which can guarantee future success. At some point all of us will reach the job that best suits our abilities and our personalities. The next step up will be a step too far. It is a wise and fortunate person who recognizes when they have reached that point.

For them, carrying out an important role successfully is better than failing at another. Some reach that moment at head of department level. For some it is the classroom. Only you know where that point is. That is why there should be no criticism of anyone who decides that deputy head is as far enough along the path that they are prepared to venture. Perhaps beyond that the undergrowth is tricky and the snakes abound. The job is important enough in itself to occupy your mind and attention. You are no lesser person for not wanting to go any further.

So some of you reading this will stay put. Others will want to move on, to test themselves, to discover whether they really are capable of leading a school community. But neither group is better than the other. Different people, different needs. What is important is that your school gets value for money for what it invests in you, no matter how long you stay.

There is an undeniable tension between discharging your responsibilities to the school and its students and pursuing your own personal goals and ambitions. You will need to keep in your mind the idea that a balance weighed too heavily either way is unhealthy. The school needs to support you but you must not forget the way in which the school has brought you to a point where you feel ready to seek promotion. Selective and considered applications are the most appropriate. Random and indiscriminate ones suggest desperation. Deputies who are out of school for weeks at a time, dragging themselves from one interview to another, are destroying their own reputation and undermining their own effectiveness.

Naturally, governing bodies are always keen to appoint those they think will move on. Ambition is seen as a good thing. It keeps you well-informed and ensures that you and your school are involved in initiatives and developments. But they do like to think that the person they have appointed has some devotion to the school where they work. It is not fair on anyone if the desire for promotion replaces a commitment to the community that appointed them. It is also the case that you do not want to give colleagues the impression of ruthless ambition, for this will undermine your effectiveness. You could be seen as someone who sets up projects and innovation merely for self-aggrandizement. Not only that, but you will also have to deal with their perception of you as a failure. If you keep on being unsuccessful then that must be because you are not as good as you are cracked up to be. Suddenly, in your absence you have been reassessed. It is not just the interview panel that has weighed you in the balance and found you wanting . . .

41 Responsibility

. . . is everything

If the title of this book, *How to be a Successful Deputy Head*, becomes a question, then the answer is quite simple. You must be true to your vocation. You must respect the job and carry out your duty. It is the same in whatever role you perform in a school. You must do what is right for the job. Never do things just because you believe it might enhance your career. You will progress in your career through the reputation you establish as someone who does the right thing, not because you are seen in the right places or on the right courses. It is in this way that you will earn the respect of your colleagues, and when you become a deputy head this is really important. You may have a title that confers seniority but you will only be able to show real leadership when colleagues have accepted you in their hearts and minds. If you are to achieve this then it will be through your commitment and performance. Do your job properly. What your school needs is an efficient, reliable and innovative leader. You are paid well to show these qualities. Aggressive careerism might eventually bring financial rewards but if such things are important to you then teaching has never been the right career choice. It is about helping to shape the future. Your obligation as a deputy is to facilitate this.

It is not that you should take the job on the assumption that you will never get another; that you are going to finish your career here. But you need to move on – at any level in the school – on the basis of doing a good job. And if promotion comes then you can move on knowing that you have made a difference and with your professional self-respect unsullied.

If you are never promoted then don't get jaundiced. You have a responsibility towards your school to lead and direct. Don't accept things as they are because that is how they have always been. Change what isn't working or what has become stale. Renew and reinvent. Remember, any change you make must be seen through properly. There is nothing teachers hate more than someone's brand-new idea that comes in with a flash and fades away just as quickly. No matter how long you are in post, the job must remain as something that is important to you. This is a really important point. The further you are promoted, the more likely you are to come across a post where finally you stick. The post of deputy head may in fact be that post. You have to accept that this is a possibility. You have done well to reach this level. In getting the job in the first place you have succeeded in a very competitive situation. Perhaps now a move won't happen for you, no matter how good you are. You might find yourself in the wrong place at the wrong time, unable or unwilling to relocate because of personal circumstances. It happens. It is not a conspiracy. You are fortunate to be in a job that so many others covet.

So if you feel that there is a danger that you are becoming stale then take some time out to assess your contribution. A mature and confident leadership team should be ready and able to facilitate this. A couple of days at home reflecting and preparing a review or a report is rarely time wasted. Walk the school occasionally and reflect upon what you see. Ask yourself these questions:

- Why am I still doing this job?
- What is important to me?
- What is important to the school?

You could ask a fellow deputy, from either within or outside the school, to assess what you are doing. They might see things that you do not. Then return the favour. Reflecting on the performance of someone you respect can often be invigorating. Without a sense of reinvention you will keep on offering only the things that you have already done. Examine the possibility of changing roles within the leadership team. A new challenge could give you the boost you need.

In the end though what you must always do is remember your responsibilities. You will have acquired experience and understanding. You must pass on this knowledge to the next generation who will one day take your place. You are part of a continuum linking past and future and you must play your part. Ensure that you have shared what you know through INSET or mentoring or even through writing a book. It is an obligation. And whatever obligations you owe to your family, you also have a responsibility to the profession as part of the continuum of knowledge that will prepare our schools to face the challenges of the future.

42 Now is the time
to say goodbye . . .

Remember me as a good thing . . .

When the time comes for you to leave you will want to go with your head held high, confident that you have served your community well. The school will be ready to move on to other things on the basis of the things that you have done. Some things will undoubtedly be changed when you have gone. Others will be preserved. Such is the way of things. But whether you are leaving to move on to another school or whether it is time to leave the profession, you should pause and consider what it is that you are leaving behind and what contribution you have made to it. Is the school a better place than it was before you arrived? What is your legacy?

You will want to think that your efforts have made a difference. Your school should be a friendly and welcoming place; it should have a positive climate, whatever that means. It is not something that can be measured objectively, but visitors to the school will know. Do the students hold doors open? Are they polite to each other? Do they treat others with kindness and respect? Your school should value relationships. It should promote cooperation and partnership at all levels. Teachers, students and leaders should acknowledge that they are all working towards a common goal. Their roles may be different and their tasks may be different, but they are all trying to achieve the same things – which are growth and success for the community. No one should feel intimidated or undervalued.

Links with the home and with the community should be well-established. Teachers should know their students and establish productive relationships with parents. Classrooms should be interesting and stimulating places where learning is valued and celebrated. The learners in those classrooms should be supported and encouraged and expectations should be high. Students should be comfortable enough to want to participate and trust the knowledge and expertise of their teachers. Lessons should start punctually and be well-prepared. Appropriate technology should be available and used properly. Your school should indeed be an aspirational place.

Teachers should have access to good-quality and appropriate training. Succession planning should be well-established. Knowledge and skills will be shared so that there is no alarming skills gap left behind when someone moves on – and you need to include the deputy in this. ·

The school will be managed effectively, with sensible use made of the most important resource of all – time. Communications will be clear and measured and information will be shared. And of course everyone should be happy to come to school.

Naturally this is an ideal, but is what you will have been striving for and you must hope that you have done something to help the school a little bit further along the road to achieving it. If you have done some of these things then you will have been a successful deputy head. It is what your job has been about. It is what you want, it is what everyone wants. There will have been many obstacles in your way but you will have always tried to keep these principles at the front of your mind. You may feel you have spent rather too much time managing situations rather than leading the school. Lunch duty, stone-throwing boys, squabbling girls, absent staff have all trampled over your plans, but you have always tried not to lose sight of the important things.

We do these things because they are important, because they touch lives, because they shape the future. It has been a duty, a responsibility, an obligation. But most importantly of all, it has been fun. And if it has been difficult then who ever said it would be easy?

43 And finally

And so, finally, we have an answer – of sorts – to the question that was asked by this book. It is not a one-word answer or one that you can learn in your head. The answer lies in the things that you do and the qualities that you show. This is how you will become a successful deputy head. You will never be deflected from the path you believe to be right and you will have the energy to make sure that the good things you perceive will happen. In order to make them happen you will:

- be organized so that goals are achieved calmly and successfully
- be responsible for everything that happens in your school
- be honest with students, colleagues and your community
- be committed to quality in all things
- be informed about the professional world you inhabit
- be measured in everything you do
- be confident that you have a vision that can shape the future for your community

If you find this list too daunting then I would suggest that this job is not the right one for you. Stay in the classroom. Life is simpler there.

If you manage all this, then you will give your colleagues the impression that your job is easy. They will believe that they can do it too. In fact, you will have been a swan in the lake of the school. Serene progress above the waterline, the consequence of frantic paddling beneath. Mind you, if you do your job badly then they will believe that there are no special skills required to do your job. 'If that clown can do it, then so can I.' There will always be others, worthy and otherwise, who will covet your job for any number of reasons.

But when others start to believe that what you are doing in your work is worthwhile and effective and want to do it themselves, then give yourself the luxury of a faint smile. Take their approval as a compliment. Indeed, there is no higher praise in the gnarled world of the staffroom. You are performing in a way that others wish to emulate. When that happens you will be able to write your own book as a guide to those who come after you.

Good luck.

Further reading

Above all else, you need to keep up-to-date. There is no ancient wisdom, chiselled on rock, recovered from sealed tombs. There are no messages, as far as we know, left on the walls of secret caves in the south of France which unravel the arcane mysteries of school management. You need to be well-informed. Whilst education is part of the political landscape then it will always be subject to constant changes. So you need to know what's going on.

Use the Internet, especially government websites. Keep an eye out for features on Teachers TV, if the channel survives.

All professional associations have high-quality journals that keep members informed. Share with colleagues the materials you find, especially if they belong to a different association. Different interpretations are always valuable. The associations all run conferences and seminars, both nationally and locally, which are often open both to members and to non-members. Keep a look out for them.

Specialist publications are available on subscription. There are very helpful ones published by Optimus Press. Of particular interest will be *Education Law Update* which I have found extremely useful.

There are many commercial publications available. You will know of them. But the most important is the oldest: *The Times Education Supplement*. Reading it includes you in the debate, puts you in contact with the great and the good. Others publications come and go, but the *TES* still remains a central voice in education. Read it regularly if you respect your profession and the people in it.

Index